SÉKOU TOURÉ

PANAF GREAT LIVES

The series provides a critical assessment of the life and work of revolutionaries who have made a significant contribution to the continuing process of world revolution, and in particular to the African Revolution. Many of them have been victims of the bourgeois information media and their achievements have been deliberately underestimated or distorted. Each book in the series is written by an author who is actively engaged in the revolutionary struggle, and who writes from an expert, often first-hand knowledge of his subject.

PANAF GREAT LIVES

Sékou Touré

Panaf
LONDON

Sékou Touré

© Panaf Books 1978, 2009.

Reprinted 2009

All rights reserved.
No part of this volume may be reproduced,
stored in a retrieval system, or transmitted
in any form or by any means, electronic,
mechanical, photocopying or otherwise,
without the prior permission of Panaf Books.

ISBN: 9780901787439

Panaf Books
75 Weston Street
London SE1 3RS

CONTENTS

		Page
	Acknowledgement	6
	Abbreviations	7
1	The Guinean Revolution	11
2	Samory Touré	18
3	French colonialism	28
4	Towards independence	42
5	'*Non*'	68
6	P D G policies and structures	86
7	Development	109
8	The anti-Guinea plot	136
9	International and panafrican objectives	163
10	The party-state	183
	Reference notes	192
	Militant poems by Ahmed Sékou Touré	
	– Tribute to Kwame Nkrumah	197
	– Revolution	199
	P D G date summary	205

ACKNOWLEDGEMENT

The publishers are grateful to President Ahmed Sékou Touré and to the National Political Bureau of the Democratic Party of Guinea for their encouragement in the production of this book, and for making available the works of the P D G from which many quotations have been taken.

Panaf also thank the Bureau de Presse de la Présidence for their cooperation and for supplying photographs.

ABBREVIATIONS

A E F	Afrique Equatoriale Française (French Equatorial Africa).
A O F	Afrique Occidentale Française (French West Africa).
B A G	Bloc Africain de Guinée, anti-R D A party in Guinea 1954–8, led by Barry Diawadou.
B D S	Bloc Démocratique Sénégalais, Senghor's party 1948–56.
B P N	Bureau Politique National (National Political Bureau).
B P S	Bloc Populaire Sénégalais, Senghor's party 1956–8.
C A P	Coopérative Agricole de Production (Co-operative of Agricultural Production).
C C	Comité Central (Central Committee).
C E R	Centre d'Education Révolutionnaire (Centre of Revolutionary Education).
C F T C	Confédération Française des Travailleurs Chrétiens (French R C group of trade unions).
C G T	Confédération Générale du Travail (Communist controlled group of French trade unions).
C G T A	Confédération Générale des Travailleurs Africains (African group of trade unions, led by Sékou Touré, which split from C G T).
C N R	Conseil National de la Révolution (National Council of the Revolution).
C P P	Convention People's Party of Ghana, founded in 1949 and led by Kwame Nkrumah until 1972.
C N T G	Confédération Nationale des Travailleurs

	Guinéens (National Confederation of Guinean workers).
COPAC	Coopérative de Production Agricole et de Consommation (Agricultural Production and Consumer Cooperative).
CUP	Comité d'Unité de Production (Party Committee of Production).
DSG	Démocratie Socialiste de Guinée (Democratic Socialist Party of Guinea) 1954–8, led by Barry III.
ECOWAS	Economic Community of West African States. Formed in 1975.
EEC	European Common Market.
ESA	École Supérieure d'Administration (Advanced School of Administration).
FAC	Fonds d'Aide et de Coopération (Aid and Cooperation Fund), successor to FIDES.
FIDES	Fonds d'Investissement pour le Développement Économique et Social de la France d'Outre-Mer (Investment Fund for the Economic and Social Development of Overseas France).
FO	Force Ouvrière, Socialist group of French trade unions which split off from CGT in 1948.
FWA	French West Africa.
IOM	Indépendants d'Outre-Mer.
JRDA	Jeunesse de la Révolution Démocratique Africaine (Youth of the African Democratic Revolution), the PDG youth movement.
MPS	Mouvement Populaire Sénégalais (Senegalese Popular Movement) pro-Ivory Coast section in Senegal, founded 1955.
MRP	Mouvement Républicain Populaire (Popular Republican Movement), French Christian Democrat Party.
MSA	Mouvement Socialiste Africain (African Socialist Movement), inter-territorial movement formed by African socialist parties, 1957.

MUR	Mouvement Unifié de la Résistance (United Resistance Movement), communist group in French parliament.
PCF	Parti Communiste Français (French Communist Party).
PDG	Parti Démocratique de Guinée (RDA section until 1958), then the independent party of the Republic of Guinea. Founded in 1947.
PRA	Parti du Regroupement Africain (African Regroupment Party), an alliance of non-RDA parties 1958–9.
PRL	Pouvoir Révolutionnaire Local (Local Revolutionary Authority).
PSF	Parti Socialiste Français (French Socialist Party).
RDA	Rassemblement Démocratique Africain (Democratic African Assembly), founded 1946. Largest group of African parties. Led by Houphouët-Boigny.
SFIO	Section Française de l'Internationale Ouvrière (French Socialist Party).
TOM	Territories d'Outre-Mer (Overseas Territories).
UGTAN	Union Générale des Travailleurs d'Afrique Noire (General Union of Workers of Black Africa).
UN	United Nations.
USA	United States of America.
USSR	Union of Soviet Socialist Republics.

I

THE GUINEAN REVOLUTION

DURING the night of 22 November 1970, Portuguese warships entered Guinean territorial waters. It was the start of an attack by hundreds of European and African mercenaries against the capital city, Conakry. The main purpose was to overthrow the government of the People's Democratic Party of Guinea (P D G) and President Ahmed Sékou Touré. For days there was fierce fighting in the streets of Conakry and around the city. But the people of Guinea were organized and armed, and the invaders were defeated. Guineans had once again surprised the world with the strength of their determination to be free.

It was the third time that Guinea had become a focus of world attention. The first occasion was in September 1958 when Guinea, alone among France's African colonies, totally rejected General de Gaulle's proposal for the Franco–African Community, and chose instead immediate independence. 'We for our part, have a first and indispensable need, that of our dignity,' Sékou Touré declared. 'Now, there is no dignity without freedom ... We prefer freedom in poverty to riches in slavery.'[1] Infuriated by the Guinean decision, the French suddenly severed all economic ties with Guinea and withdrew administrative personnel, teachers, doctors and technicians. Seemingly unprepared for independence, and summarily cut off from French assistance, it was widely thought that Guinea could not possibly survive as an independent state. But de Gaulle, and those who predicted that Guinea would soon beg to return to the French fold, were wrong. Guinea not only survived, but achieved as the years passed, an international stature quite out of proportion to its size, population or economic development.

In March 1966, Guinea again attracted the attention of the world news media, when Kwame Nkrumah stepped from an aircraft at Conakry airport to a 21-gun salute and an ecstatic welcome from the people of Guinea. Only days before, his C P P government had been overthrown by a military coup while he was on a mission to Hanoi with proposals for ending the war in Vietnam. The western news media was happily prepared to consider Nkrumah finished. But Sékou Touré and the P D G at once sent a message inviting him to Guinea where he would be able to continue the African revolutionary struggle. 'The Ghanaian traitors,' said Sékou Touré in his welcome address, 'have been mistaken in thinking Nkrumah is simply a Ghanaian ... He is a universal man.' Amid the cheers of the people of Conakry, Sékou Touré proclaimed Nkrumah co-President of Guinea.

The Guinean welcome to Nkrumah, the fact that he remained in Conakry from 1966 until his illness in 1971,[2] and did some of his most important work there, immeasureably enhanced the position of Guinea in the panafrican world. At the same time, it increased the reputation of Guinea as a militant and progressive state.

But quite apart from these periodic occasions when news from Guinea seems to take the world by surprise, there are other reasons why this comparatively small West African state is of particular interest. Guinea, unlike other former French colonies, broke completely with France at independence thereby becoming one of the few countries at independence to sever ties with the former colonial power. After independence, Guinea continued to be the odd-man out as far as the French-speaking countries of West Africa were concerned. For a time, the republic of Mali under the leadership of Modibo Keita pursued similar policies to Guinea, but after his overthrow in a military coup in 1968, Guinea was once more unique among former French colonies in her independent stand.

Guinea, unlike most other newly-independent states, has had the same leadership since independence. In a continent which has come to be characterized by military coups this is indeed an achievement. Other former French colonies, notably Cameroon, Senegal and Ivory Coast, which have also retained the same civilian government since independence[3] have, unlike Guinea, had the protection of close French cooperation, and in some territories French troops stationed there. For example, under a defence agreement there are some 1,300 French troops stationed in Senegal. In the case of Cameroon, where the French colonial government brutally suppressed the Union des Populations du Cameroon (U P C), the party which pioneered the fight for independence, French military assistance has kept in power the government of Ahmadou Ahidjo, ever since independence in 1960. Hundreds of U P C members fled abroad, and most of the original leadership have been eliminated. Reuben Um Nyobe was killed by French colonial troops in 1977. On 3 November 1960, Felix Moumié was poisoned in Geneva almost certainly by a French secret service agent. Ernest Ouandie was shot by firing squad in the centre of Bamileke on 15 January 1971.

The P D G has had no such foreign protection, and has, through the support of the people, developed an infinitely stronger political image and a reputation for progressive policies. The strategic position of Guinea, the richness of its mineral resources, and the unique nature of its revolutionary development, make it one of the countries of Africa of greatest interest to the world.

It is a country in which the people are supreme and where there can be said to be mass participation in government at all levels. Furthermore, the political ideas of the P D G and of Sékou Touré, and his personal style of leadership have had a profound impact on developments throughout Africa and specially on the panafrican and liberation movements, which Guinea has always supported.

Yet in spite of the political continuity there are many exposures of plots or intended plots. Large numbers of Guineans live outside Guinea, notably in Ivory Coast and Senegal. Sékou Touré, in broadcasts and speeches constantly warns the people to be on their guard to repel invaders, and to seek out hidden enemies from among themselves. Between 1958 and 1976, no less than six major plots were exposed, each of them involving foreign powers, Guinean dissidents living outside Guinea, and local reactionary elements. First came the so-called Teachers' Plot in 1961, to be followed in subsequent years by the Traders' Plot, the Plot of the Loi Cadre, the Plot of Kaman Diaby and Fodeba Keita, the mercenary invasion of 1970 and the Foulah Plot of 1976, the first to involve an ethnic group rather than a class or individuals.

All were successfully dealt with by the people of Guinea, yet independent Guinea has never, it seems, been able to afford to relax vigilance. For scarcely a year goes by without rumours of further plots and invasion threats. The people of Guinea appear to be faced with a 'permanent plot'. An editorial in the P D G newspaper *Hoyoya* of 12 September 1971 endorsed this view: 'If we won our independence without any violence, it still remains true that the threats and attempts at colonial reconquest constituted since 1958 a sword of Damocles suspended over the young Guinean nation.' Sékou Touré put the matter into the same perspective in his speech of 26 July 1971, when he said:

> On September 28, 1958, imperialism was astonished to find a people who no longer wished to accept the least vassalage, the slightest complex, the least dependency on anyone.
>
> The Guinean people's action for independence and dignity, though it be in poverty instead of opulence in slavery, was considered by the imperialist powers to be an injury etched on their monstrous countenances, a challenge they wish to take up at any price, to the great misfortune of the peoples of Africa and the world.
>
> Thus the colonial powers, supported since then by other powers, determined to maintain our people and our wealth in the chains of exploitation and oppression, began to foment a permanently anti-Guinean plot, which is in truth the anti-African plot.
>
> From 1958 to 1970 we have never ceased being the target of the criminal enterprises of imperialism and colonialism.

What is the true nature of the situation in Guinea? What has been achieved by the P D G since independence in 1958? Can Sékou Touré survive the anti-Guinea plot? And can the P D G survive him? How can some of the apparent inconsistencies in the actions of the Guinea government be explained? Why, for instance, does the P D G which proclaims socialist policies, allow foreign capitalists to assist in developing Guinea's resources? What is the role of the party-state of Guinea in the unfolding African Revolution?

Only with a study of the historical background of French colonialism, and of developments in Guinea since 1958 seen within the broad context of African and world political, economic and social processes can a start be made at demystification of what some regard as 'the Guinea enigma'.

For various reasons there has been at times a virtual *cordon sanitaire* surrounding the country. News which has leaked out has often appeared contradictory and distorted. For example, in the months following independence, it was widely believed in the West that Guinea was being swept helplessly into the communist orbit, since countries of the socialist world were the first to recognize the new state and to offer assistance. The socialist policies pursued by the P D G lent further support for this view. When, for reasons which will be examined later, the Soviet ambassador was suddenly expelled from Guinea in 1961, and western influences seemed to be strong for a time, Guinea was said to have 'come in from the cold', and to have changed direction. Misinformation about what happens in Guinea has continued to lead to misunderstanding and erroneous conclusions. To some extent this has been due to the deliberate spreading of false information by Guinean dissidents opposed to the P D G. Another factor has been the difficulty experienced from time to time by foreign observers in obtaining permission to visit Guinea. Ever since independence, the Guinean people have felt threatened by elements both inside and outside the country hostile to the P D G, and this has necessitated the maintenance of strict security measures, and at times the closing of frontiers. But the P D G has not pursued policies of isolationism. On the contrary, it has been determined to play an active, positive role in international and panafrican affairs.

There is news about Guinea in French language newspapers, magazines and books, though much of it has tended to be hostile and biased. There are also the yearly published works of the P D G and collections of Sékou Touré's speeches, which contain detailed information about the policies and the performance of the P D G. But for the non-French readership there has been surprisingly little published about Guinea, and most of it very limited in scope. This dearth of reliable information has been a factor in causing some of the misconceptions about the country and its people. But what is difficult to understand has been the failure to grasp or publicize what information is available. Those who write about Guinea so often fail to let the P D G speak for itself. The party has made its position and policies clear, yet these statements are insufficiently quoted, and instead writers put forward their own impressions without giving the readership the benefit of making up its own mind from source material. In Guinea no attempt is made to conceal true situations. Problems and difficulties are openly discussed and recorded in the works of the P D G. There is much flexibility and experimentation concerning methods, and economic and political structures, and these also are public knowledge. They have been arrived at only after protracted discussion in the various levels of party organization.

It is unusual for parties and leaders to reveal their hands so openly. From the start there was no mystery about the broad policies Sékou Touré and the P D G intended to pursue. At Guinea's independence, Sékou Touré declared that the country was non-aligned. In addition, he stated quite clearly that the capitalism which characterized colonialism was neither an appropriate nor acceptable economic and social form of organization for independent Guinea. 'When people ask us if we are for capitalism or socialism, for the East or for the West, we invariably answer that what we consider first and above all is the Africa we intend to liberate from foreign domination, sickness, misery and ignorance.'[4] The P D G rejects capitalism because it 'does not correspond with our stage of development', and because it is based on greed and exploitation. 'Guinea needs capital,' said Sékou Touré, 'but not capitalism.'[5] As for ideology, 'I say that philosophy does not concern us, we have concrete needs.'[6] Thus no static tactical positions are taken. The P D G is constantly adapting and progressing in the light of changing conditions, and as a result of public discussion. There is a fluidity, a preparedness to experiment, to modify and even to abandon concepts and political and economic structures if they prove unsuitable in practice. Overriding realities and the needs of the people are key. This is why emphasis is placed on the priority of political considerations in order to achieve the consistent ultimate objective of a unified and just society not only in Guinea but in the whole of Africa and the rest of the world. There is concentration on the general political interest rather than on specific sectors or purely economic interests. 'Political economy,' according to Sékou Touré, 'is not the adaptation of political action to economic action; on the contrary, it is the use of economic activities for political ends.'[7]

It is the purpose of this book to examine the true nature of the Guinean experience from on the spot observation, and using source material. Any assessment of the Guinean revolution can only be a limited one while the P D G under the leadership of Sékou Touré continues. Doubtless many developments may yet take place which could cause the revision or abandonment of any conclusions reached. However, sufficient time has passed for it to be worthwhile attempting an interim progress report. If some of the more common questions asked about Guinea can be discussed, and glaring misconceptions exposed, then perhaps a helpful purpose will have been served.

General de Gaulle, referring to Guinea in a press conference on 23 October 1959, a year after independence, said: 'Guinea is for us a growing entity, and we do not know into what it will develop.' After nearly twenty years a similar remark might still be made. But there would be no excuse for uncertainty about the direction of its development. 'Don't judge us by what others say, or even by what we say,' Sékou Touré told the press in 1962, 'but only by what we do.'

2

SAMORY TOURÉ

THE name most associated with early African resistance to French colonialism is that of the Almamy Samory Touré. For eighteen years, until he was finally defeated in 1898, Samory Touré fought against the French and became a legend in his lifetime for the way in which he governed the vast Madinka empire, and for his skill and tenacity in war. This is the renowned great-grandfather of Ahmed Sékou Touré through his maternal grandmother, Bagbé Ramata Touré, a daughter of the Almamy.

In view of the importance of Samory Touré in the emergence of the modern state of Guinea, it is necessary to look at the Samory experience and to outline the historical processes which preceded it. For the people of modern Guinea still continue the Samory tradition in their determination to remain free, and in their reputation for political maturity and militancy.

When Samory Touré was born in about 1830, the people of the forest and savannah areas of the hinterland of West Africa, as well as in the coastal regions, were accustomed to Europeans and to their merchandise. Opinions differ as to when exactly the first European contacts were made with Guinea. French historians have claimed that ships from Dieppe reached the Guinea coast in 1364, but there is no documentary evidence to prove this. What is certain is that during the fifteenth century, in the reign of the Portuguese ruler Prince Henry the Navigator, Portuguese seamen established contact with West Africa and explored over 1,500 miles of coast from Cape Bojador to Sierra Leone. In 1434 Gil Eannes rounded Cape Bojador and nine years later, Nuno Tristam returned to Portugal with the first cargo of twenty-nine slaves. In the same year, 1443, another Portuguese seaman, Antam Goncalves, brought back to Lisbon the first small quantity of gold dust from the Rio de Oro.

A papal decree gave Portugal exclusive rights to the west coast of Africa. Further voyages followed, by Tristam, Diniz Diaz, Cadamosta and others. Cadamosta, a Venetian captain in the service of Portugal, sailed 250 miles up the Senegal river in 1455, and spent some months trading cloth for small quantities of gold. The following year, he travelled sixty miles up the Gambia river. But he failed to achieve his objective of getting in touch with the gold market of Timbuktu.

For a time, after Henry the Navigator's death in 1460, royal enthusiasm for trade and exploration waned. But it was not long before further voyages were made when the initiative passed into the hands of merchants bent on developing a rich trade with the coastal peoples of West Africa. With improved ships the equator was reached in 1471, and the Congo estuary by Diego Cam in 1482. Diego Cam made two further voyages to the Congo, and established friendly relations with the local paramount chief, Manicongo. The voyages of Diego Cam virtually completed the European exploration of the West African coast. The remaining area was visited by Bartholomew Diaz on his return from his epic voyage round the Cape of Good Hope in 1487.

For the next fifty years or so, the Portuguese monopolized the trade of the Guinea coast. But then the English, Dutch, French and Danish began to compete, and to build trading posts and forts along the coast, for example at Gorée, Cape Coast, Elmina and Calabar. These and other trading depots became centres for trade in slaves, ivory, gold and commodities such as pepper, gum and dyestuffs.

It is possible that the name 'Guinea' derives from the kingdom of Ghinea, Genni or Jenne, which existed in the eighth century around the source of the Niger river. Or it may derive from the ancient kingdom of Ghana (or Ghanata), the oldest known state in western Sudan, originating in the third century. Between the seventh and twelfth centuries, Ghana was a powerful empire extending, at its height, from Timbuktu to Bamako, and even as far as to the Atlantic Ocean. At one time it included Jenne.

For many years, 'Guinea' was the name given by Europeans to the whole West African coastal region from the Gambia to the Congo. The name also described the gulf formed by the bend of the coastline eastwards and then southwards. 'Guinea' first appeared on maps in the middle of the fourteenth century, though the name did not come into general use until the last part of the fifteenth century. The early European traders gave different names to various parts of the Guinea coast according to what goods were produced there. The area extending some 500 miles eastwards from Sierra Leone was called the Grain Coast, because it was from there that traders obtained large supplies of pepper, known as 'grains of paradise'. The Ivory Coast was so called from the elephant tusks it supplied. To the east of the Ivory Coast was the Gold Coast and the Slave Coast.

Largely because of navigational difficulties, the area comprising modern Guinea was not visited by European traders of the sixteenth to the eighteenth centuries as frequently as regions to the north and east. But slave traders did call there from time to time, usually as a last resort after having been driven away from other parts of the Guinea Coast. Remains of the forts they built can still be seen, mainly on the islands off the coast of Guinea.

It was not until they recovered Gorée in 1815 that the French showed special interest in the region of modern Guinea. At that time, the British, who were already in Gambia and Sierra Leone, were investigating the possibilities of extending their activities along the rivers south of Senegal, and in the Fouta Djallon, the mountainous area in the north-west part of Guinea.

The extensive areas of forest and savannah lands stretching inland from the coastal regions of West Africa, remained largely unaffected by Europeans until the nineteenth century. But in 1827, the Frenchman René Caillé started his journey from Boké to the west of Conakry, towards Timbuktu. From 1838 onwards, French naval officers, L. E. Bouët-Villaumez and his successors, made detailed studies of the area. Colonel Louis Faidherbe was appointed governor of Senegal in 1854. Under his administration, strenuous efforts were made to consolidate French influence, and many treaties of protectorate were signed. It is estimated that between 1845 and 1897, more than thirty treaties of 'friendship and protection' were signed between the French and local chiefs. When in 1881 the Fouta Djallon was brought under French 'protection', the British abandoned the idea of linking up their colonies of Gambia and Sierra Leone. Britain recognized the right of France to the littoral as far south as the basin of the Melakori in 1882.

It was during the last part of the nineteenth century that the European 'scramble for Africa' began in earnest. Britain, Germany, France, Portugal, Spain, Belgium and Italy proceeded to divide up most of Africa between them. Ancient boundaries were disregarded and peoples divided as artificial mini states were created to serve the interests of the colonial powers. In West Africa, Britain and France succeeded in grabbing most of the territory. Germany, which had attempted to acquire a protectorate at Conakry, gave up its claims in 1885. The following year, the northern frontier of Guinea was settled by agreement with Portugal, which had interests in the area. Finally, in 1904, the boundaries of the modern state of Guinea were completed when the Los Islands off the coast near Conakry, were ceded by Britain to France in return for the abandonment of French fishing rights in Newfoundland waters. Until 1890, the newly-gained French territories forming Guinea were administratively part of Senegal. They then became a separate colony called Rivières du Sud. Five years later, the name was changed to Guinée Française.

While European influence spread inland from the coastal regions of West Africa, the Arab conquest of North Africa in the seventh century had laid the area open to Islamic penetration by way of the Saharan trade routes. Probably a decisive point was the conquest of the Ghana Empire by Muslims of the Murābitūn movement in 1076. During the next nine centuries, Islam spread throughout West Africa, filtering through the forest belt and to the coastal regions of

Guinea, Senegal, Dahomey and Nigeria, but remaining at its strongest in the desert and savannah lands to the north.

During the eighteenth century, certain Peuhl tribes had taken over the Fouta region of Guinea and had created an Islamic state of nine provinces. It was from the Islamic states of the West African hinterland that European colonialists encountered the stiffest resistance. Leaders such as Ahmadu Lobo, who established an Islamic state in Massina, in modern Mali, about 1810; and Samory Touré, who ruled a large empire in Upper Guinea towards the end of the nineteenth ventury, identified Islam with opposition to colonialism. For colonialism was synonymous with Christianity and European culture. The fact that Islam still remains the predominant cultural tradition in northern Nigeria, Niger, Mali, Guinea, Senegal and Mauritania, is testimony to the effectiveness of local resistance to social and cultural aspects of French and British colonialism.

Samory Touré was not born a Muslim. He was a Diula, a group of the Mandinka people who inhabited an area of the western Sudan, which had once formed the ancient empire of Mali. The region bordered the Fouta Djallon to the west, and to the east the Mossi and Asante kingdoms. Although nominally a Muslim people, the Diula practised pagan rites along with their Muslim faith. They were a people noted for their skilled craftsmen and for their merchants who traded with European merchants along the River Senegal, and in Monrovia and Freetown. At the beginning of the nineteenth century, they lived in villages or in small towns. But by the middle of the century, some of the Diula towns were expanding into the neighbouring areas and becoming sizeable states. Kong, one of the most important of Diula towns, had by 1860 developed into the largest Mandinka state. Kankan, Odienne and Sikasso had also, by the mid-nineteenth century expanded to become quite large states.

It was at this stage in the history of the Mandinka that Samory Touré began his remarkable rise to power. Starting as a trader in gold and cattle, he gradually formed an army, initially from among his personal friends and relations, and soon began to establish his authority over a large area from

Milo to Dyon. He adopted the warrior title of *Faama*. By about 1870, having brought the small states of the Wassulu area under his control, he established his capital at Bisandugu. There he abandoned the old name of *Faama* and adopted instead the Muslim title *Almamy*. He had found Islam to be a unifying force, and so set out to make it the religion of his empire. By dividing his enemies and attacking each one separately, Samory was able to capture Kankan, conquer the Sisé, and to become ruler of the largest empire that the Mandinka had ever known.

Samory's army was noted for its rigid discipline, its modern weapons and fighting skill. He studied the different guns used by European troops, and organized groups of workmen able to copy the Gras and Kropatschek rifles. It was essentially an infantry army, but cavalry units were used from time to time with great effect. Large numbers of the soldiers were warriors captured in war and given their freedom in return for service. Others were levied from conquered territories, or were mobilized on a yearly basis. It is estimated that Samory's army numbered some 100,000 men, though not more than about 20,000 were under arms at one time since the men were needed on the land to maintain agricultural production. The army was divided up into combat units, unlike most other African armies of the time which were organized on tribal or village lines. Most of the weapons and horses bought for the army were obtained through the selling of gold, ivory and slaves. The latter were mostly either rebels or prisoners of war. Probably some 3,000 a year were sold for this purpose to Arab traders in the north.

Samory inspired great devotion and loyalty, and was almost worshipped by his soldiers. He never risked their lives needlessly. It was his policy to avoid large battles with European troops since their superior artillery would inflict heavy casualties on any massed formations. He was a superb tactician, employing guerrilla methods. Attempts were always made to save the wounded. Those who were maimed and could not fight again were given work to enable them to support themselves and their families.

The military reputation of Samory is matched, or even superceded by his record as an administrator. He was seen as a natural leader of the Mandinka, a unifier, who had done much to revive the former glory of the ancient empire of Mali. Coming from a humble family himself, Samory was determined to destroy the power of the chiefs and privileged groups in society. His first concern was education so that everyone would have a fair chance to achieve the highest positions in the state. Education was made compulsory for the children of state officials. In the army, basic literacy was taught and the way was open for anyone to rise from the lowest to the highest position. Religious leaders took their places alongside political and military officials. Images, sacred groves and other relics of feudal and superstitious traditions were replaced with mosques and schools. For Samory's administration aimed to establish Islamic values.

The empire was divided into 162 cantons, each canton consisting of twenty or more villages. The cantons were grouped into ten provinces, and from village to province, authority was vested in traditional, military and religious personnel. Village and canton chiefs, chosen by traditional methods, held very little real authority. The power of village chiefs was limited by the village Imam and by Samory's representative who was responsible for the raising of troops and supplies for the army. In the cantons, power was exercised by the military administrator, and alongside him were traditional and religious leaders. Governing the provinces were close associates or relatives of Samory Touré, assisted by a military chief and a scholar. Samory himself was the political and religious head of the empire as well as the supreme commander of the army. He was assisted by a state council composed of political, religious and military leaders from the provinces.

Samory's empire is generally considered to be the most efficiently administered of any West African empire of the nineteenth century. It was unusual at that time for emphasis to be placed on unity and the ending of privilege based on tribe or class. Although much of the time the Mandinka were at war, either fighting the French or other African peoples, very substantial progress was made in building some of the more important aspects of a modern Muslim state. There was a unified and effective administration, a high standard of education and social well-being within the context of Islamic laws and customs.

But it is Samory Touré's record as a courageous fighter against the French for which he is most remembered in independent Guinea. Realizing that the French intended to seize the whole of the Sudan, Samory tried for some time to play off British and French colonialists in the hope that he might avoid open confrontation until he was better prepared. But the British government did not wish to come to terms with Samory, preferring instead to bargain with the French for concessions in other parts of Africa. When, therefore, open war between the French and the Mandinka began in 1891, Samory had to face the French alone.

Before then, there had been numerous French expeditions into the regions of what is now Upper Guinea and Mali. The first contact was made with Samory when in February 1882 Lieutenant Alakamessa visited him at Gbèleba and warned him not to attempt to take Kènyéran, an important market town in the Fyé valley. Samory disregarded the warning and in November besieged the town. In the meantime, Colonel Borguis-Desbordes had led an expedition towards the Niger, intending to take Bamako. But due to lack of reinforcements he had to abandon the idea, and instead attempted to relieve Kènyéran. The French forces surprised Samory but were too late to save the town, and they were compelled to retreat.

During the next few years, Samory's forces continually harassed the French forces as they probed further and further into the interior. It was a running battle of skirmishes and sieges over a vast area. The French, with their extended lines of communication, were perpetually short of provisions and reinforcements. Samory's forces made the most of their predicament, ambushing and attacking them as they pushed their way through the difficult and unfamiliar terrain; and besieging them when they took refuge behind the walls of forts.

The reputation of Samory grew as a tenacious and elusive enemy. For although the French with their superior artillery frequently defeated his forces they could never win a decisive victory because Samory seldom committed more than 1,000 men against the French at any one time. While part of his army concentrated on attacking the French in small-scale encounters, other troops looked after the civilian population, organizing the mass evacuation of territory as the French advanced. Villages were burned down and crops destroyed so that the French occupied a deserted land, and faced shortages of food and ever-lengthening, hazardous supply lines.

By 1896, Samory had been gradually compelled to abandon the first Mandinka empire, and a second empire had been formed to the east with a new capital at Dabakala. The second Mandinka empire was not as strategically placed as the first. The Buré goldfields had been lost, and also the valuable trade links with Freetown. In addition, the southern areas of the empire were vulnerable to French attacks from Ivory Coast. To the north and east were unfriendly African kingdoms, and Asante, which the British had occupied in 1896. Samory found himself short of guns and horses. He had, therefore, to increase the export of slaves to the north in order to compensate for the lost wealth which he had depended upon for the purchase of military supplies. At the same time, he had to depend more and more on the output of army equipment from the state workshops.

In 1898, the French captured Sikasso and Bobo Dioulasso, cutting off the northern trade route. French armies were advancing from north, west and south. To the east, Samory's retreat was cut off by the British in Asante. He had, therefore, to abandon Dabakala. Shortly afterwards, when Samory was hard-pressed on all sides and desperately short of supplies, the French were able to trick him into surrendering. They promised him safe conduct to his home village, but he was seized by French forces and deported to Gabon. There he died of pneumonia two years later, in 1900.

The fight put up by the Mandinka under the leadership of Samory Touré was the longest and most effective of any resistance to the European invaders of West Africa. If others had followed the Mandinka example and joined forces with Samory the colonization of West Africa might have been much longer delayed, though it is doubtful if it could have been prevented in the long run owing to the superiority of European weapons and technology. As it was, local jealousies and antipathies played into the hands of the colonizers.

Samory alone among West African rulers seemed to grasp the full significance of European ambitions. Not only did he lead Mandinka resistance to the invaders for eighteen years, but he united the Mandinka people as never before, and administered one of the best-governed empires of the time. There is a striking parallel between the courageous fight of Samory Touré and the Mandinka, and the stand of his descendant Sékou Touré and the Guinean people in their determination to be independent and to create a unified society. It is not surprising that the body of the Almamy Samory Touré now rests in a tomb in the centre of Conakry reserved for the nation's heroes.

3

FRENCH COLONIALISM

AHMED SÉKOU TOURÉ was born on 9 February 1922 in Faranah, near to the source of the River Niger. His father was Alpha Touré and his mother, Aminata Fadiga. Although descended from what has been termed the 'sword nobility' they were poor peasants, and the young Sékou Touré grew up without social privileges. As a child he heard much about the campaigns of Samory Touré and was proud to be a member of the same family. To the north-west of Faranah, between Kankan and Nzérékoré is Kérouane, Samory Touré's base and the site of the fort he built in 1890. The ruins remain, now known as Tata de Samory. The Almamy had died in 1900, and there were old folk in Faranah who could give eyewitness accounts of the armed struggle against the French. In addition, there were the mosques, schools and other evidence to keep alive memories of the great Mandinka empire. But superimposed on the traditional society were all the structures and pressures of the French colonial system. During his childhood, therefore, Sékou Touré was exposed on the one hand to the powerful influences of the Samory tradition, and on the other to the harsh realities of foreign occupation.

Guinea at the time of Sékou Touré's birth was, and still is, a predominantly Moslem country, and the young Sékou Touré began his education at a Koranic school before attending the Faranah primary school and then the regional school at Kissidougou. At school, Sékou Touré quickly gained a reputation for hard work. He was one of the brightest pupils, interested in everything, and a voracious reader. Teachers and schoolfriends describe him in those days as a thoughtful, modest and compassionate boy, who was extremely sensitive to any injustice. In class he was always one of the first to put up his hand to answer the master's questions. Some of his schoolfriends named him the 'little wizard', though not to his face for fear of offending him. They remember how he used to help the less intelligent members of the class by telling them the solutions to problems so that they might escape punishment. Then, realizing that he was doing them a disservice, and that they must be encouraged to work harder, he organized them into work groups. In the evenings after school they would gather around a forest fire and the more talented boys would teach the less able ones. Sékou Touré took charge of mathematics, and according to one of his comrades, he taught easier methods of mental arithmetic than those learned in class.

It was when he was in school at Kissidougou that he began to display the qualities of leadership and dedication to just causes which was soon to bring him as a young man into the forefront of the struggle for national liberation. His strong sense of justice caused him in 1936 to lead a protest against the headmaster. A boy had died as the result of a snake bite while working in the headmaster's garden. The headmaster, who had no right to make boys work in his garden, had refused to admit that the cause of the boy's death was a snake bite.

Sékou Touré further antagonized the school authorities when he persistently refused to learn colonial history. He scorned the history master, and tore out pages from his textbook which disparaged African heroes such as Samory Touré. No amount of caning affected his determination never to learn a falsified history of Africa. A schoolfriend, Ibrahima Bayo, has described an occasion when pupils were told to repeat what they had learned about Samory Touré. When it came to Sékou Touré's turn, he refused. The master, Fodé Bokar Maréga, asked him the reason, and Sékou Touré replied: 'The history that is taught about Africa appears to me untrue. Concerning Napoleon Bonaparte, we are told that he was a great hero and a brilliant strategist, and that he conquered Europe. When it comes to Samory Touré, we are taught that he was ignorant and bloodthirsty. What is the truth? Bonaparte, in order to conquer Europe, killed many thousands of people. If Bonaparte is a hero so also is Samory. If Samory was bloodthirsty, Bonaparte was more so.' This incident caused Sékou Touré's name to be erased from the list of pupils to go on to the École Primaire Supérieure (E P S). In making his reports the headmaster wrote against the name of Sékou Touré: 'An intelligent pupil, hardworking, punctual, but a danger to France. If admitted for further education it would be advisable to direct him to the École Georges Poiret.'[1] To the astonishment of everyone, because Sékou Touré was known to be a brilliant pupil, he was duly admitted to the Georges Poiret technical school. He accepted the decision because the school was in Conakry, where he thought he could best pursue the political work to which he had already dedicated his life.

Between 1936 and 1937, he was moved from one section of the school to another after various confrontations with the school authorities. The following year, he was made to do metalwork. But he was expelled in mid-course for leading a food strike. From 1939–40, he did various jobs. For a time he worked as an apprentice builder, then in an iron foundry. But he continued to educate himself through correspondence courses, until in 1940 he became an employee in the Compagnie du Niger Français. He was then eighteen years old, and already showing much of the spirit which was to bring him into direct conflict with the colonial authorities.

In 1941, he passed an exam qualifying him to work in the Post and Telecommunications Department. Four years later, he formed the first trade union in Guinea, the Post, Telegraph and Telephone Workers' Union. He went on to help form the Union Cététiste des Syndicats de Guinée and became its secretary-general in 1946. In the same year, he joined the Treasury department and was elected secretary-general of the Treasury Employees' Union. There, his political activities brought him into conflict with the French colonial administration. He not only lost his job, but spent a brief period in prison. On his release, he determined to devote most of his time to trade union work.

Sékou Touré then, grew into manhood at a time when Guinea had been a colony of France for nearly half a century. On the first of August 1889, the Rivières du Sud had been freed from the administrative control of Senegal, and two years later, in December 1891, the French colony of Guinea was formally created with Dr Noël Ballay as the first governor. Under his administration, which lasted until 1900, Guinea was divided into *cercles* each under a French commandant. The *cercles* were divided into cantons administered by local chiefs appointed by the governor. Unlike the British colonialists who at local level employed methods of indirect rule through traditional chiefs, the French operated a system of direct rule through chiefs chosen and paid by the administration. In addition, the *cercles* and cantons did not necessarily correspond to traditional jurisdictions.

Originally, the French empire south of the Sahara consisted of only three small trading stations in Gabon, Ivory Coast and the two settlements of St Louis at the mouth of the Senegal River, and Gorée, an island in Dakar harbour. But at the time Sékou Touré was born, the French West African empire consisted of the territory at present covered by Mauritania, Mali, Senegal, Guinea, Ivory Coast, Upper Volta, Benin and Niger. These formed an administrative unit based on Dakar and directed from Paris.

With the expansion of the French empire it became clear that it was a primary aim of the French government to bring colonies into closer integration with France. Not only were colonies to become a part of France in the political sense, but the colonial people were to be transformed into Frenchmen. Political progress in the colonies, as far as the French were concerned, was to be measured by the advance in the direction of greater integration. The height of political advancement of colonial people would lead not to self-government but to the goal of full participation of Africans as Frenchmen in the government of a greater France.

The French colonial policy of assimilation was based on the assumption that French culture and nationality was superior to that of the colonized peoples, and that it could and should be adopted by them. France alone among

European colonial powers set out to assimilate its colonial subjects until they would culturally, legally and politically become Frenchmen.

The origins of the policy of assimilation and its racialist undertones, are well illustrated in a remark said to have been made at the beginning of the eighteenth century by the French king Louis XIV to a prince from Ivory Coast: 'There is no longer any difference between you and me, except that you are black and I am white.' At the time of the French Revolution, nearly a century later, Danton and Delacroix managed to persuade the Convention to vote that 'all men without distinction of colour, who live in the colonies, are French citizens and enjoy all the rights guaranteed by the Constitution'. However, this measure was repealed a short time afterwards by Napoleon, and it was not until 1848 that colonies were given representation in the French National Assembly. They were to be administered like provinces of France. The French language, educational system, law, and basic social, economic and political patterns were to be applied so that gradually the colonial people would be totally assimilated into becoming an integrated part of the French nation.

But although assimilation was a comprehensive colonial theory, the purpose being to mould the colony and the colonized peoples in the image of France, it was a theory which applied in practice to only a small minority of France's colonial subjects. This was the élite class of evolués, those who were considered to have absorbed a sufficient amount of French culture to qualify for French citizenship. Evolués were granted political, economic and social privileges similar to those enjoyed by the middle class in France. Yet as Frantz Fanon found out when he went to France in 1944, evolués were treated as second-class citizens. In Fanon's book *Black Skin, White Masks*, he shows how all the theoretical talk about equality and assimilation meant very little when it came to being absorbed into French society. He found that evolués met racial prejudice everywhere. Often it was revealed in the manner in which Frenchmen spoke to Africans. Although the evolué might be a member of the professional class and speak French perfectly, Frenchmen would invariably address him in 'pidgin nigger', thus showing that he was not accepted as an equal. Fanon noted that the French created a hierarchy amongst colonized peoples. Those from the Caribbean, for example, occupied a higher rung on the social ladder than those from Africa. Fanon wrote that he had known people born in Africa who pretended to be West Indians, and West Indians who were annoyed at being thought to come from Africa. During the Second World War, West Indians were absorbed into French army units, while recruits from Africa were placed in special platoons and battalions.

The evolué, alienated from the mass of his people, and only superficially accepted into the society of the white man, was therefore in a dilemma. Either he had to suffer the humiliation of knowing his acceptance was only superficial, or he had to try to enhance his position and ingratiate himself with his own people by joining his fellow evolués in developing new concepts such as négritude. Through the theory of négritude, Africa's past could be idealized. European culture could be replaced with black culture, but an African culture tailored to meet the needs of the evolué.

The early followers of négritude were grouped round the journal *Présence Africaine*, founded in 1947 by the Senegalese writer Alioune Diop. Leading promoters of négritude were Aimé Césaire, the West Indian writer, and Jean-Paul Sartre, the French political theorist whom Fanon as a young man so much admired. In taking a rightful pride in the culture of Africa, the advocates of négritude distorted the facts to fit in with their own social and political aspirations, and in doing so, developed what Kwame Nkrumah described as a 'pseudo intellectual theory'.[2] He declared that it served as a bridge between the African foreign-dominated middle class and the French cultural establishment, and he denounced it as 'irrational, racist and non-revolutionary'.[3] Sékou Touré holds much the same view of négritude, regarding it as the philosophy of an élite which grew out of the French colonial policy of assimilation. At the African cultural festival (F E S T A C) held in Lagos in 1977, Sékou

Touré sent a message to be read at the opening ceremony in which he strongly denounced négritude as a bourgeois class ideology based on Francophonia and Francophilia. It was, he said, a part of western cultural imperialism. Sékou Touré stressed the realities of African culture, its role in the liberation struggle, in the consolidation of African unity and in economic development. In other words, African culture is not a vague 'something' which can be separated from political, social and economic contexts. It is part of the African personality and as such has a vital role to play in the African Revolution.

The leading exponent of négritude in Africa is Leopold Sédor Senghor of Senegal, one of the most assimilated of French-speaking Africans, an evolué par excellence, who can envisage no future without France. 'Politically, we work to make the West African a French citizen,' he declared in 1937.

Senegal was the first French colonial territory where the doctrine of assimilation was seriously applied. There were large numbers of French merchants and government officials living in St Louis, Gorée, Rufisque and Dakar, the four towns which came to be known as the *Quatre Communes* (Four Communes). The towns were governed in much the same way as a province in France. Both black and white inhabitants were subject to French educational and administrative systems. Municipal councils were set up in 1872 and a General Council in 1879. Elections were, as in France, based on universal male suffrage. In theory, both Europeans and Africans could vote and stand for election. Similarly, both black and white were entitled to the protection of their rights under the French judicial system. The Four Communes were represented in the Chamber of Deputies in Paris by a locally elected deputy. Rural Senegal and other West African territories of France were a purely executive responsibility. The French government could legislate for them by decree.

Real power was in the hands of the French Governor-Generals of the two administrative areas Afrique Occidentale Française (A O F) with its capital in Dakar, and Afrique Equatoriale Française (A E F), the capital of which was Brazzaville. Both A O F and A E F were financially autononous and had their own budgets. Only military expenditure and loans were underwritten by France. The Governor-Generals headed a centralized hierarchy of administrators descending through the territorial governors to *commandants de cercle* and *chefs de subdivision*. Below these were the so-called 'customary' *chefs de canton* and *chefs de village* who were appointed by the French administration. Although these local officials were said to be traditional administrators, this was in fact far from the case. They were merely subordinate administrators responsible to colonial officials. The French gave these local nominees virtually despotic power since they were appointed and removable only by the colonial administration, and not by the African people. According to African custom, a chief is strictly controlled by democratic or oligarchic assemblies. If he does not give satisfaction he can be removed and replaced by another.

The key figure in the French colonial hierarchy was the *commandant de cercle* who was in charge of roads, law and order, health, agriculture, and certain other local matters. This official may be compared with the District Commissioner in the British colonies.

While there was much in common between the administrative structures set up by the various colonial powers, there were points of difference which characterized each. A feature of French colonialism, for example, much resented by Africans was the *indigénat*. This was the name of a group of provisions in the French criminal code which enabled administrators to inflict punishment on Africans without reference to a court of law. In some cases, administrators were authorized to impose penalties as severe as deportation or imprisonment for up to ten years. However, by 1940, the term of imprisonment which was usually imposed was restricted to about a week, with the alternative of a 100 franc fine. Another aspect of French colonial 'justice' was the so-called native penal code under which a large category of actions which were legal for French citizens were criminal offences when committed by African subjects.

Even more resented by France's colonial subjects was the system of forced labour. This was widespread throughout the French territories in West Africa. Africans were forced to work, for example, on railways, roads, rubber, cocoa and coffee plantations. There was a high mortality rate among workers many of whom were forcibly transported to places of work long distances from their homes.

In general, the French policy of assimilation failed. For although the French succeeded for a time in establishing political and economic domination over their colonies, they were never able to carry out effective cultural assimilation. A people's culture is deeply rooted, and even if it were possible to wipe out one culture and replace it by another, the process could only begin to take effect over a very long period of time.

In West Africa, the French found that their attempt to impose European concepts of the private family unit and the individual ownership of land met with stiff opposition. The way of life of the majority of Africans was based on the extended family system, and on the collective ownership of land. Furthermore, most of the people were Moslems, and therefore governed by Islam and the Koran. As Muslims they tended to be polygamous and this automatically disqualified them from complete assimilation. For to be fully assimilated and to become an evolué, a person had to be a monogamist and subject not to the Koran but to French legal codes. Here again, the French ran into difficulties in their attempt to accelerate the process of assimilation. For education, which might have countered Islamic influences, was largely in the hands of Christian missions, and therefore only a small percentage of the population attended school. Most of the schoolchildren went to local Koranic schools where they received a basic Islamic education. But only a very small number of children progressed farther since the French secularized education in 1903 and this meant there were fewer private schools. In 1934, it is estimated that some 60,000 children were at school in French West Africa (F W A) out of a population of about fourteen million. This figure may be compared with the 315,000 schoolchildren in a population of twenty-five million in British West Africa, where education remained largely in the hands of the Christian missions. Apart from the scarcity of schools, those that did exist tended to be concentrated in certain areas. Senegal had more than any other French territory in West Africa. In 1947 it is reckoned that 10 per cent of African children were receiving primary education in Dahomey, 12.4 per cent in Senegal, and only 1.3 per cent in Guinea.

The percentage of children receiving secondary education in F W A was far smaller. The school attended by most of the leading personalities of F W A, with the notable exception of Sékou Touré, was the École Normale William Ponty founded in Saint Louis in the north of Senegal in 1903. The school was transferred in 1913 to the island of Gorée, and moved again in 1937 to Sébikotane on the mainland about forty-six kilometres from Dakar.

Education in F W A had a limited purpose. The missions required teachers, catechists and lay preachers. The colonial administration and the large European trading companies wanted clerks. Apart from the École William Ponty in Senegal, there were only two other secondary institutions of high standing in the whole of West Africa during the colonial period. They were Achimota College in the Gold Coast, and Fourah Bay College in Sierra Leone. A few Africans went to Europe or the U S A for further education at their families' expense. But this was very rare.

If Sékou Touré had attended the École William Ponty like so many of the leading personalities of F W A, it is possible that he might not have become such a vehement opponent of colonialism, and such a strong upholder of African freedom and dignity. Sékou Touré never aspired to evolué status. He is not a product of French culture, or for that matter of any foreign civilization or ideology. He saw the trap of assimilation. His style has always been totally African. 'We have,' he said, 'our own message to deliver, our own human resources to pool with the human resources of modern society, the characteristic values of our civilization to contribute to the value of other civilizations.'[4] He added: 'Africa cannot agree ... to become an organic extension of any system of states or ideologies whatsoever.'[5]

In 1935, that is after some forty-five years of French rule in Guinea, there were only 6,558 schoolchildren in a population of two million. There were thirty-four elementary schools, nine regional schools, two orphanages, one apprentice school and two agricultural trade schools, one at Labé and the other in Kankan. Secondary education was non-existent.

Assimilationists were to discover that while educational opportunities served to promote French culture, they at the same time stimulated African political awareness. Africans began to condemn the concept of racial and cultural inferiority implied in the policy of assimilation. They demanded genuine equality and the right to live according to their own customs and civilization. In the face of growing African resistance the French were gradually forced to modify their policy of assimilation. In 1916, Senegalese rights as French citizens were confirmed, and these rights were extended to their descendants. It meant that people were 'naturalized' collectively and not on an individual basis as hitherto. This achievement was largely the result of the efforts of Blaise Diagne,[6] the first black African to sit in the French Chamber of Deputies in Paris. He had been elected deputy in the 1914 elections to the French Parliament. About 50,000 Senegalese were made French citizens in 1916. This number grew to around 80,000 by 1946, a very small percentage of a total population of F W A of more than ten million.

During the first quarter of the twentieth century, the aim of many Africans in F W A was to obtain French citizenship, not because they admired French culture, but because it was only through 'citizenship' that they could enjoy the same rights and privileges as Frenchmen, and be treated with respect. As 'citizens' they could vote, and be voted for, at elections. They had the right of protection under French justice, and qualified for equality of opportunity in education and employment, though in practice this did not mean very much. Non-French citizens on the other hand, had no such rights. They were openly treated as inferiors and were completely at the mercy of local French administrators.

As far as Guinea was concerned at this time, the French

policy of assimilation had nothing like the impact it had in Senegal. For although the territory was governed as part of the administrative unit of A O F, there were few towns of any size, and a relatively small number of French settlers. In theory, any French colonial subject could become a full citizen. In practice, few availed themselves of the so-called 'privilege' because it meant renouncing the right to live by African customary law. Outside the Four Communes, 'citizen' remained virtually synonymous with 'European'. Like other colonies, Guinea was only developed in those areas which served the economic interests of the colonial power. The economy was based initially on rubber and oil palm products. Between 1909 and 1910, rubber production was at its peak. It accounted for more than 60 per cent of the total value of exports, most of which left the country through the port of Conakry.

There were few roads, most of them unpaved, and only one railway running from Conakry to Kankan. These were constructed mainly to enable cash crops to be transported to the coast, and to facilitate troop movements. As time went on, feeder roads were built to link up towns along the railway lines. These increased in number as transport lorries came to be used to carry produce from peasant producers direct to the exporting companies, or to the depots of middlemen.

For the majority of people who were engaged in subsistence agriculture, colonialism brought additional burdens in the form of taxation, forced labour and military recruitment. While Europeans enjoyed a privileged tax position, and the big foreign trading companies were practically immune, the average peasant paid out a large part of his income in direct taxation. The introduction of a market economy and currency circulation had undermined traditional trading patterns. At the same time, the development of commerce was not related primarily to the need for money to buy imported goods, but in order to be able to pay taxes. In 1897, the payment of a head tax of two francs was imposed for all Africans above the age of eight. By 1928, revenue from the head tax accounted for over 70 per cent of

Guinea's revenue. The percentage dropped to 46 per cent during the Second World War when Guinea supplied many raw materials required by the allies. But in 1956 the head tax for every person between the ages of fourteen and sixty ranged from 812 to 1,085 C F A francs; and this on a population whose average annual per capita income was estimated at about 10,000 C F A francs.

The export trade was dominated by European trading companies, chief among them being the Compagnie Française de l'Afrique Occidentale (C F A O), the Société Commerciale de l'Ouest Africain (S C O A), and the Compagnie du Niger Français. These had depots in the interior where they employed other traders as middlemen. At first, much of the trade in rubber and palm oil products was carried out on a barter basis, the merchants supplying imported goods from their warehouses in exchange for raw materials. Soon, Syrian and Lebanese merchants moved in and rapidly began to monopolize the purchase of rubber by paying cash instead of insisting on an exchange of goods. By 1905, it is estimated there were some 700 Levantine merchants in Conakry alone.

Meanwhile, the infrastructure required to meet the growing needs of commerce was developed. Following the building of the first pier at Conakry in 1895, other improvements were gradually made to the port to facilitate the import and export trade. The railway from Conakry to Kindia was extended to Mamou in 1908, to Kouroussa in 1910 and to Kankan in 1914. All these developments had the result of increasing the importance of Conakry at the expense of Bamako, Freetown and Nunez, which had hitherto attracted the bulk of the trade of the Fouta and Upper Guinea.

The production of rubber in Guinea declined sharply between 1910 and 1913 as prices fell due to the coming into production of large rubber plantations in other parts of the world. Guinea's rubber production was down to 190 tons in 1934. By then, Guinea had become a leading banana producer. From a production of only seven tons of bananas in 1903, some 26,000 tons were produced in 1934. Apart from oranges and a relatively small production of coffee, palm oil, rice, oil seeds, ground nuts and sesame, there was very little else grown. Subsistence agriculture, and cattle-raising mainly in the Fouta Djallon were virtually the sole productive sectors. A few fruit canning factories comprised the only processing industry in the country.

The existence of gold, diamonds, iron ore and bauxite was well known. But their exploitation was of scant interest to the French since France itself was an exporter of ores, and French firms were unwilling to risk investing in large-scale ventures which might not prove profitable. Small quantities of gold continued to be mined at Siguiri, and diamonds in Upper Guinea, but there was inadequate investment and traditional methods of production continued to be used.

There was in fact very little to show on the credit side for French colonialism in Guinea. Economic development, communications, health, housing, education, were at a level barely sufficient to serve the basic requirements of the colonial administration and of foreign fiorms. As far as health was concerned, there was as late as 1955 only one hospital for the whole of Guinea. This was built in Conakry in 1901. There were two ambulances, twenty dispensaries or medical depots, and fifteen maternity homes or midwifery centres. Schools, medical care, houses were only available to the privileged few. As the Guinean writer J. Suret-Canale put it: 'The peasant continues to eat and labour in the same way as his ancestors, except that he labours harder and eats less.'[7] Sékou Touré, addressing the U N General Assembly in 1959 went farther: 'Colonization,' he said, 'may put up buildings and factories, bridges and ports, but it can only crush and divide the peoples by degrading man.'

4

TOWARDS INDEPENDENCE

WITHIN fifteen years of the ending of the Second World War in 1945, almost the whole of West Africa was freed from colonial rule. It was the culmination of mainly non-violent campaigning by African nationalist movements, and the result of long-term liberation processes which had been set in motion ever since the colonial period began. For although open, armed resistance to European occupation ended for a time as the colonial powers forcibly established their rule, opposition continued and developed new forms.

Ideas of national liberation had been discussed in political organizations in the colonies since the last part of the nineteenth century. Typical of early nationalist movements in British colonies in West Africa were the Aborigines Rights Protection Society and the National Congress of British West Africa. But in F W A, where there was stricter control, political activity was largely confined to the Four Communes. Between 1848 and 1852, and then continuously from 1872, the Four Communes sent a deputy to represent them in the National Assembly in Paris, and in 1916, the inhabitants were granted confirmation of French citizenship mainly as a result of their loyalty during the First World War.

A number of events and developments in world affairs which occurred during the first half of the twentieth century accelerated liberation movements not only in Africa, but also in the Middle East and Asia. Notable among them were the 1917 revolution in Russia, the two world wars, the entry of the communists into Peking in 1949, and the war in Indo-China. The vulnerability of western powers was exposed as resistance grew to all forms of oppression and exploitation.

Between the two world wars, communist parties were

formed. One of the most significant was the Communist Party of France (P C F). The P C F played an important role in the French wartime resistance movement, and as a result emerged from the war with its reputation greatly enhanced. Like other communist parties, the P C F supported colonial independence movements and trade unions, and set up 'study groups' in the colonies to help to create national consciousness. There had developed in many of the colonies a strong labour movement which in Guinea was merged with the national party through the leadership of Sékou Touré, who headed both the P D G and the trade union movement.

A further significant factor in the rise of national consciousness was the return home of many thousands of colonial soldiers who had fought on the side of the allies during the Second World War. They had seen the early defeats of British and French armies. France collapsed in 1940, and in the Far East the British were defeated by the Japanese. Singapore fell in February 1942, and Rangoon the following month. The British prime minister, Winston Churchill, promised the Indian people independence in return for their cooperation in the war. Furthermore, it became necessary to make a clear statement of allied war aims. Churchill and the U S President, Franklin D. Roosevelt, meeting on a warship in mid-Atlantic drew up the Atlantic Charter, article three of which declared: 'the right of all peoples to choose the form of government under which they live'. It went on to state that the two leaders wished to see 'sovereign rights' restored to those who had been forcibly deprived of them.

The colonial troops in supporting the allies believed therefore that they were fighting for freedom. But after the war, the ex-servicemen returned to their homes disillusioned, having discovered that the promised freedoms did not apply to them. However, their wartime experience and knowledge of conditions in other parts of the world enabled them to play a very important part in national liberation movements.

When France collapsed in 1940 there would have been no Free French territory had it not been for the French empire. General de Gaulle in a broadcast of 18 June 1940, declared that France remained undefeated and that mainland France would be liberated through the allies and from Free French bases in the colonies. A few years later, French troops suffered defeat in the Indo-China war during which some 100,000 Frenchmen were killed. A new mood of confidence inspired colonial peoples as they saw the weakness of the colonial powers and realized how much they depended on the human and economic resources of their colonies. Africa had become an area of international importance, and among the colonial peoples there were those who were determined to make the most of the new situation to press for political change.

While liberation movements in the British colonies campaigned for self-government, nationalist movements in F W A tended to aim at greater integration with the colonial power. This was hardly surprising in view of France's colonial policy of assimilation, and the fact that most leading politicians of F W A received their political experience and training not in local legislatures as in British colonies, but in the French National Assembly. They were led there for some time by two of the consistently most enthusiastic supporters of France, Houphouët-Boigny of Ivory Coast and Leopold Senghor of Senegal, both of whom became ministers in the French government.

Administrators in F W A for a time supported the collaborationist Vichy government. In A O F and Togo, the French administrations did not rally to de Gaulle until November 1942, after the allied invasion of North Africa. But A E F joined Free France in 1940. Both A E F in 1940, and A O F in 1942 followed up their support of Free France with changes in administrative personnel and a marked swing towards progessive policies. A most significant turning point was reached in 1944 with the Brazzaville Conference. On 30 January 1944, de Gaulle as chairman of the Free French Committee of National Liberation presided over the opening session. Present were Frenchmen, colonial governors and officials, a few trade unionists and a bishop. Guinea was unrepresented because at that time the post of governor was unoccupied. Dominating the proceedings was Felix Eboué, born in French Guiana and the African governor of Chad in

1940, who was the first in Africa to respond to de Gaulle's appeal of 18 June 1940. De Gaulle appointed him Governor-General of A E F in recognition of his support.

The conference was summoned to discuss French colonial policy, and in particular, French interests in sub-Saharan Africa. The aim was to determine on what practical basis it would be possible to construct a French union. For two and a half years, Brazzaville, the capital of A E F had also been the capital of the 'French government'. Troops trained in A E F bases crossed the Sahara and under the command of General Leclerc fought in the final battles of the North African campaign. It is estimated that more than 100,000 Africans fought in Free French armies. But it was not only the strategic and military importance of the war effort in F W A that incurred the gratitude of de Gaulle and the French, but also the vital economic support of the colonies in supplying essential commodities. It was felt that there needed to be a new spirit of reform in France's colonial policy both to show recognition of the part played by the colonies in the allied victory, and to try to confirm France's domination over them. For at that time the principle of ultimate independence was not considered. As de Gaulle himself declared at the conference: 'the aims of French colonial policy exclude any idea of autonomy and any possible future self-government for the colonies'. This was made quite clear when the conference endorsed the views of René Pléven, Free French Commissioner for the Colonies, when he said:

> We read at one time or another that the war must be ended with what is called a liberation of the colonial peoples. In the great colonial France there are neither peoples to liberate nor racial discrimination to abolish. There are populations which feel themselves to be French and which wish to take – and to whom France wishes to give – a greater and greater part in the life and democratic institutions of the French Community. There are populations which we mean to lead, stage by stage, to personality, for the most mature and political freedoms, but

who do not mean to understand any other independence than the independence of France.[1]

It was agreed that the colonies should enjoy a large measure of administrative and economic freedom, and should be increasingly associated with the management of public affairs. The colonies were to be represented in the Constituent Assembly to be summoned at the end of the war when a new constitution would be drawn up for the Fourth Republic.

It was clear, however, that it would not be sufficient merely to increase the number of colonial senators and deputies in Paris. Members of the conference spoke of a 'colonial parliament' or federal assembly which would 'strengthen and guarantee the unbreakable political unity of the French world, while respecting the local life and freedom of each of the territories'.[2] Until this time, the Four Communes were the only parts with a deputy in Paris, and the only towns in F W A with elected town councils.

There was to be a clear distinction between the powers of the central government and those of the individual colonies. Within the colonies, the *conseils d'administration* were to be replaced by a subdivisional and regional council of notable evolués,[3] representing the traditional élite; and representative assemblies containing Europeans and Africans elected by universal suffrage 'wherever such a possibility is recognized'.[4] These assemblies were to be empowered to vote the colonial budget, but otherwise to be advisory only. In other words, each colony was to develop representative institutions but to be indissolubly linked to France.

Other recommendations of the Brazzaville Conference referred to social and economic matters. More jobs were to be open to Africans 'but for the time being the higher grades carrying authority can only be open to French citizens'.[5] There was to be a uniform African penal code. *Indigénat* punishment was to be abolished at the end of the war. Members of the conference called for a pension scheme for workers, a six day week and an eight hour day. On the much resented system of forced labour, the conference declared the principle of the absolute superiority of the freedom of labour, but agreed that it would take at least five years to apply this principle in practice. Even then, young men were still to be liable for a year's conscripted labour as an alternative to military service. Trade unions might be encouraged; and a rapid expansion of education and state aid to industries was recommended.

In the months which followed the Brazzaville Conference, several reforms were carried out. A new system of recruitment and training for colonial administrators was introduced. A uniform penal code for Africa was drawn up, and various systems of customary jurisdiction were reorganized. Mobile medical units were formed. Taxation in kind, and compulsory *corvées* were abolished. The formation of trade unions was authorized. In view of the fact that most of the population of F W A was engaged in subsistence farming this affected only a small minority of mainly urban workers – but it was a relatively politically-aware sector of the population, and in Guinea proved to be a decisive force in forming national consciousness. Wireless and telegraphic services between the colonies were extended. The improvement in communications generally formed part of the plan to develop the economies of the colonies in accordance with the Brazzaville recommendations. As far as education was concerned, a special conference was held in Dakar in July 1944, and a 20-year plan drawn up for A O F. There were to be 50,000 new primary schools, 200 upper primary schools, and 75 *écoles normales africaines* to train some 50,000 extra teachers.

On the implementation of the political recommendations of the Brazzaville Conference, progress was slower. In February 1945, the French government set up a special commission to work out procedures for colonial representation in the Constituent Assembly. Chairman of the commission was Gaston Monnerville from Guiana who had been a member of the Chamber of Deputies before 1940. Two Africans were co-opted. They were Senghor and Sourou Migan Apithy of Dahomey, both of whom had been in Europe since the beginning of the war. In fact, Senghor had lived in France almost continuously since 1928. Neither he nor Apithy could by any stretch of the imagination be said to be in close touch with their countries or to represent them. They did, however, strongly oppose the draft project before the commission which divided the territories of the French empire into three categories. The first were the 'states', or former protectorates. The second were departments of the French Republic; and the third were 'countries over which France must continue to exercise its domination'. The colonies of F W A were to be included in the third category. Senghor and Apithy opposed the suggestion on the grounds that African representatives in the Constituent Assembly were to be voted for by an electorate of only a small minority of French 'citizens'. It was eventually decided that a mere thirty-three colonial deputies were to sit in an Assembly of 586 members A referendum was to be held at the same time as the election to give the Assembly constituent powers. While 'subjects' could vote in the election, only 'citizens' were to be eligible to vote in the referendum. The franchise, however, was so limited that a mere 203,000 people, less than 1 per cent of the population of the whole of the French administered territories south of the Sahara, had the vote. In Guinea, only 18,100 people in a population of some 2,125,000, that is 0.9 per cent of the population was able to vote. In each African constituency there were to be two seats, one of them reserverd for 'citizens' and one for 'subjects'. In most territories, therefore, one half of the representation was effectively reserved for the small European population.

Elections were fixed for 21 October 1945, and the thirteen territories of Afrique Noire were grouped into eight parliamentary constituencies. Three had their own. They were Ivory Coast, Guinea and Cameroon. The remainder were grouped. For example, Senegal was paired with Mauritania. In the event, Senghor and Amadou Lamine-Guèye were elected as deputies for Senegal; Houphouët-Boigny won in Ivory Coast; Apithy in Dahomey; and in Guinea, Yacine Diallo was elected. There were in all, eight Africans elected to the Constituent Assembly. They were all evolués, and three out of the four West African deputies had been educated at the École Normale William Ponty. The African deputies entered the Constituent Assembly in Paris as members of the French union and not as delegates seeking independence for their countries.

When the Assembly met in the Palais Bourbon in November 1945, there were three main parties: the Communist Party with 152 seats; the Mouvement Républicain Populaire (M R P), a left-wing socialist organization founded by Roman Catholic resistance leaders, with 150 seats; and the Section Française de l'Internationale Ouvrière (S F I O), the French socialist party. In addition, there was the Union Démocratique et Sociale de la Résistance (U D S R), an anticommunist resistance group which included René Pléven; the Radicals with twenty-eight; the Mouvement Unifié de la Résistance (M U R), consisting of members who wanted to work with the communists but who were not members of the Communist Party; and sixty-four independents who supported more or less conservative policies.

One of the African deputies, Amadou Lamine-Guèye of Senegal, a joint founder of the Senegalese socialist party, tried to form a *bloc Africaine* in the Assembly and to affiliate with S F I O. However, he was unsuccessful, and he together with Senghor, Yacine Diallo of Guinea, Apithy (Dahomey), and Jean-Félix Tchicaya of Zaire (then the Congo) joined S F I O. Houphouët-Boigny of Ivory Coast and Fily-Dabo Sissoko of the Soudan joined the M U R; and Manga Bell Doula (Cameroon) joined the M R P.

In view of the anti-imperialist policies of the Communist Party it might have been expected that the African deputies would be its natural allies. But while communist deputies assisted, they did not try to enrol them into the Party. Instead, they encouraged them to join the M U R. This was because the Communist Party considered Africa not yet ready for communism. In their view, the preliminary stage of bourgeois national liberation had to come first. This attitude to some extent explains why French communists in Africa formed study groups rather than party cells. Their short-term aim was to stimulate nationalism rather than class consciousness. So although African leaders such as Boigny and Senghor on many occasions found themselves supporting the French communists, it was not from ideological conviction but because the P C F representing the French proletariat in its struggle against capital, was also the party most deeply committed to anti-imperialist policies.

The French multi-party system enabled the African deputies to exercise considerably more power in Paris than their numbers justified. For there were many occasions when their votes could be decisive. Although on the whole it was difficult for them to press for colonial reform when members of the Assembly were usually more concerned with domestic issues, some reforms were nevertheless achieved. In December 1945, a decree abolished all provisions by which administrators could impose prison sentences and fines without the judgement of a court. At about the same time, the C F A franc was created to provide some protection for the colonies from the devaluation of the French franc. In January 1946, 'colonies' as such ceased to exist. De Gaulle resigned and under the new government headed by the socialist leader Félix Gouin, the colonies became *Territoires d'Outre Mer* (Overseas Territories, T O M), and Marius Moutet became the first French minister of T O M.

In the months which followed, further colonial reforms were passed. A decree abolished arbitrary arrests, and fines imposed collectively on communities. Forced labour was abolished throughout T O M. Then in April 1946, the Investment Fund for Economic and Social Development (F I D E S) was established to provide long-term loans for overseas development projects. Between 1947 and 1957, French territories in Africa received nearly 200,000 million C F A francs in credits from F I D E S, much of it being spent on medical services, education and economic infrastructure. This expenditure only represented 1·5 per cent of France's national income, and made a negligible impact.

As discussion proceeded in France in 1946 over proposals for a new constitution, differences appeared between Left and Right on the colonial question. The Left was generally in favour of a federation of free and equal partners, each territory joining the French Union voluntarily and deciding its own relationship with France. The Right, on the other hand, advocated a federation with central organs strong enough to prevent secession, the exclusion of overseas deputies from the French National Assembly, and a federal citizenship distinct from that of France. In the end, a compromise was reached. The Right accepted token overseas representation in the National Assembly, and African territories of France became members of the Fourth Republic.

In June 1946, when a Second Constituent Assembly was elected, the M R P emerged as the largest single party with 169 seats, and the socialists and communists therefore no longer had an automatic majority when voting together. Georges Bidault replaced Gouin as prime minister, and under his leadership there was a swing back to a tougher colonial policy. Public opinion in France was ready for this largely because of events in Madagascar, Indo-China and Algeria. In Madagascar, liberal reforms had been met with anti-French demonstrations and a general strike for further reform. In Indo-China, French recognition of the Republic of Vietnam had resulted in Ho Chi Minh's government demanding recognition of its authority in Cochin-China, Annam and Tongking. The freeing of nationalist leaders in Algeria had led to their winning eleven out of the thirteen second-college seats in the election.

It was in this situation that de Gaulle re-emerged. In a speech in June 1946, he declared that the French Union should be federal in structure, and that while federal and national legislatures should be distinct, the executive should be both federal and national. The implication was that colonial territories which were not yet states within the federation would be governed by presidential decree.

According to the constitution of October 1946, A O F, A E F, Somaliland and Madagascar were territories d'Outre Mer and formally included within the Fourth Republic. Togo and Cameroon were designated 'associated territories'. In practice, they were treated in the same way as T O M, but their governors were called High Commissioners of the Republic, and their Assemblies were named Representative Assemblies, while those of T O M were called General

Councils to make them appear like Departments in metropolitan France. Both T O M and the Associated Territories were to be represented in the French National Assembly and the Council of the Republic. Deputies to the National Assembly were to be directly elected. But there was to be a very limited franchise. Only $3\frac{1}{2}$ per cent of the total population in A O F could vote, $2\frac{3}{4}$ per cent in A E F, $1\frac{1}{2}$ per cent in Cameroon and 1 per cent in Togo. The total number of deputies for Africa was 24 in an Assembly of 618 members. In the Council of the Republic, the Senate, there were 315 members, 19 of which were from A O F, 8 from A E F, 3 from Cameroon, and 2 from Togo. These were elected indirectly by the General Councils and Representative Assemblies on a double voting roll system. The powers of the Territorial Assemblies were very restricted. For although they voted local budgets there were several important categories of expenditure which they could not refuse. As far as the federal budgets of A O F and A E F were concerned, these were voted by the two Great Councils which met in Dakar and Brazzaville for a few weeks annually. Inevitably, tension developed between territorial and federal interests. The Councils in Dakar and Brazzaville were viewed with suspicion by the Territorial Assemblies intent on developing increased powers over matters of local concern, and strengthening the African voice in the French Union.

Moves were made by African deputies in the French Assembly to form a permanent alliance of all African political movements, and invitations were sent to leaders of 'French' African territories and to French political parties summoning them to a congress to open in Bamako on 18 October 1946. Marius Moutet, Minister of T O M, at once tried to persuade people not to attend. Two months earlier, speaking before the Constitutional Commission, he had asked the question: 'Does France really consider herself as uniting 110 million souls, or rather does she wish to retire into herself, considering herself only as a people of forty million? Will France be a great power or will she not?' Moutet was here expressing the post-war decision of French leaders to base the recovery of France on the preservation of the empire.

While the British talked of partnership in a Commonwealth, the French talked of a Community of 110 million Frenchmen.

When the Bamako Congress opened 800 delegates had assembled, most of them from West Africa. Lamine-Guèye, Senghor, Yacine Diallo and Tchicaya did not attend. While Apithy, Boigny and Gabriel d'Arboussier, a colonial administrator from Gabon travelled to Bamako in an aircraft lent for the purpose by the communist Minister of Aviation. It was at this congress in Bamako in October 1946 that the *Rassemblement Démocratique Africaine* (R D A) was formed to represent the whole of A O F, and A E F, the aim being to seek to secure genuine equality for Africans within the French Union. A Committee of Coordination under the chairmanship of Boigny was formed at the same time to bring about the union of political parties within each territory, and to prepare the way for their fusion into the R D A. Sissoko, Apithy, Tchicaya, d'Arboussier and Mamadou Konaté (Soudan) were appointed vice-chairmen. The R D A, therefore, was not a political party so much as a broad alliance of parties and groups able to present a unified African voice within the French Union. In keeping with the Francophile views of most of its founders, Boigny spoke of the indestructible attachment of Africans to republican and democratic France. Fittingly, the proceedings ended with the singing of the Marseillaise.

Between 1946 and 1950, the R D A worked closely with the French Communist Party, not for ideological reasons but because of its persistent anti-colonial line. By 1950, the R D A had 700,000 members and was the largest political organization in Africa. It was the dominant party in Guinea, Ivory Coast, Mali, Cameroon and Chad, and the leading party in Volta, Niger and Congo (Brazzaville).

But already at the time of the elections of November 1946, it was clear that there were serious differences between African nationalists which would diminish the chances of achieving a really united African front. In Paris, Sissoko joined the socialist group, while Konaté joined the M U R. None of the African socialists joined the R D A, whereas all the ten R D A deputies were affiliated to the M U R. The socialist group in the new Assembly included such notable figures as Lamine-Guèye, Senghor, Sissoko, Yacine Diallo, Silvandre, Horma Ould Babana (Mauritania), Jean-Hilaire Aubame (Gabon) and Jules Ninine (Cameroon). Of the ten R D A deputies, three, including Boigny, represented Ivory Coast. The other seven were, Apithy (Dahomey), Tchicaya (Moyen-Congo), Konaté (Soudan), Hamani Diori (Niger), Gabriel Lisette (Chad), Martin Aku (Togo) and Mamba Sano (Guinea). In Guinea, the vote was split between the R D A and the socialists, each having one seat. The socialist Yacine Diallo drew his support mainly from the chiefs of the Fouta Djallon; while the so-called Socialist Party of Guinea supported Mamba Sano.

The close relationship between the R D A and the C P F began to cool when the Communist Party left the coalition government of Paul Ramadier in March 1947. This came at a time when full-scale war was raging in Indo-China, a war which was to last seven and a half years; and when there had been a revolt in Madagascar leading to the arrest of three Malagasy deputies in Paris. Opinion in France was hardening against any further moves which might encourage colonial peoples to demand more freedom. The P C F which had openly supported the nationalists both in Indo-China and Madagascar suffered a decline in popularity enabling Ramadier to dismiss P C F members from the cabinet. However, R D A members in the Assembly continued to vote with the P C F until October 1950 when Boigny finally severed the alliance.

The decision of the R D A to break communist affiliations was due in part to the reign of terror launched by colonial administrators against the R D A at this time. Leaders were arrested, demonstrators imprisoned, newspapers closed down, and many chiefs who belonged to the R D A deposed. In addition, elections were rigged to result in the defeat of R D A candidates. There were particularly severe disturbances in Ivory Coast. On 30 January 1950, thirteen Africans were shot by French troops at Dimbokro. Two days later, a decree was issued temporarily banning R D A meetings throughout Africa. So severe and brutal was the suppression of nationalism in the French colonies at this time, that the sternest measures taken by the British to stifle national liberation movements in their colonies seemed mild in comparison.

Members of the R D A retaliated with strikes, boycotts and civil disobedience campaigns, but by the end of 1951, so ruthless had been the suppression that the R D A was virtually silenced for a time. When at length it re-emerged under the leadership of Boigny some five years later and won the 1956 elections in every colony except Senegal and Mauritania, it was an R D A which had been successful because it was prepared to compromise and to cooperate with the colonial administration. Henceforth its influence and power rapidly declined, and with this decline there resurfaced the influence of Senegal in F W A. Before 1946, Senegal had been accustomed to adopt a leadership role in West Africa. But Senegal's political and economic dominance suffered temporary eclipse with the rapid rise to importance of Ivory Coast. Opposition to the R D A came mainly from Senegal where Senghor organized a group of opposition parties throughout F W A against the R D A. This group was known as the *Indépendants d'Outre Mer* (I O M). Members voted as a bloc on all African issues in Paris. Their purpose was to bring about a federal constitution for the union and greater powers for Territorial Assemblies.

The decline in importance of the R D A brought an increase in the power of its national parties. In Guinea, where the Parti Démocratique de Guinée (P D G), had been formed in 1947 as the national section of the R D A, Sékou Touré was emerging as a politician and trade union leader of considerable stature. Civil servants in the communications and postal service, and railway workers had been the first to organize within the framework of the French Confédération Générale du Travail (C G T). They were followed by wage earners in the public services, employees in trading firms and artisans in small enterprises of various kinds. For a time there was virtually no cohesion between them, until early in 1946, when a union was formed in Kankan to include all labour sectors in the region. In March

1946, the C G T sent a labour mission to F W A which convened a conference at Dakar attended by thirteen European and twenty-one African delegates. It was here that the Union des Syndicats Confédérés de Guinée (U S C G) was formed, and it was decided that each of its vocational unions should be affiliated with its metropolitan counterpart. Two delegates were chosen to represent the new organization at the 27th C G T congress to be held in Dakar in 1947. They were Sékou Touré and Maurice Guignouard, a European. But while Sékou Touré supported the degree of unity which had resulted in the formation of the U S C G, he nevertheless regretted the failure of many workers in the private sector to join the new confederation. There existed still the Catholic Confédération Française des Travailleurs Chrétiens (C F T C) and the socialist Force Ouvrière (F O), though neither had anything like the membership of the CGT.

Initially, the main objectives of the labour movement were for wage increases, improvements in working conditions, paid holidays, family allowances, compensation for accidents, and equal pay with Europeans for the same work. In general, Africans earned three to four times less than Europeans with similar qualifications. The demands were ostensibly purely economic, but in reflecting the anti-colonial struggle they were basically political. 'We do not fight for a salary demand,' declared Sékou Touré, 'we fight for power.'[6]

Between 1945 and 1952, a wave of strikes took place. Notable among them was, first, a three month strike of railway workers which started in December 1947 and lasted until mid-March 1948. The strike which was a federal one was supported by all railway workers in the A O F-Togo colonies. It gained the support of trade union organizations and of the people as a whole, and particularly of the P D G. 'All the newspapers of the party and of the trade union organizations controlled by it set themselves the main goal of ideological education and training of the people to prepare them for the struggle.'[7] In this way, many anti-colonial actions were initiated in the various sectors by traders, peasants, wage earners, ex-servicemen and others.

Another important strike occurred in June 1950 when wage earners in the public sector were joined by those in private employment. This strike resulted in fierce repression by the colonial administration aimed at intimidating party leaders, many of whom, including Sékou Touré were thrown into jail. But the people's reaction was so strong that the colonial governor, Roland Pré, was compelled to release him after three days. The party's journal *Coup de Bambou* (No. 27), had contained the warning: 'Harm our comrade, and all the workers not only in Conakry but throughout the whole of Guinea will rise up.' The struggle continued unabated with the party calling for industrial action and the unions responding as an integral part of the politico-economic front to end colonialism and to bring social and economic transformation.

There were further strikes in 1951 and 1952 at a time when the mining of bauxite at Kassa and iron at Kaloum was getting under way. Mass rallies were organized in major towns throughout Guinea in order to mobilize and educate the people. According to Sékou Touré: 'From 1952, the party became more consistent and gathered strength. Its original methods of penetration of the society, of permanent contact and ideological education enabled it to establish a larger and larger social basis, whereby it called for more important strikes.'[8]

A significant factor in the increasing political consciousness of workers was *L'Ouvrier* (The Worker), the first workers' newspaper in Guinea. Sékou Touré had become a very accomplished journalist. He wrote not only most of the paper himself, but also produced it on a copying machine. In *L'Ouvrier*, he regularly denounced the rapacity of capitalism, and drew attention to the miserable living conditions of the African people. He was preparing them for the most significant episode in the great struggle for the liberation of Guinea, the 72-day strike which was to take place between 21 September and 30 November 1953.

In November 1952, Sékou Touré and his colleagues on the Co-ordinating Committee of the A O F–Togo Trades Union movement presided over the Dakar Trades Union conference. It was at this conference that a resolution was passed calling for a general strike throughout A O F. 'So wide was the scope of the workers' determination that the colonial authorities understood in time that the strike was likely to deal a fatal blow to the colonial system.'[9] The Overseas Labour Code was rushed through the French parliament in December 1952 though according to Sékou Touré 'a confidential telegram was sent to all colonial governors instructing them to "defuse" the strike, but not to implement the Labour Code. Telecommunications workers in Conakry who were all militants of the P D G passsed on the secret message to the P D G, and this helped to harden our position in exacting the implementation of the Labour Code.'[10]

The general strike was launched in all A O F colonies. But through methods of intimidation, the French managed to defeat the workers' movements in all colonies except Guinea. 'We in Guinea had pledged not to surrender until victory.'[11] As before, the people of Guinea regarded the strike as 'the supreme means of manifesting vigorously their anti-colonialist determination'.[12] Landlords with workers as tenants, charged no rent while the strike lasted; families which supplied meals to workers refused to accept payment. Peasants at Forécariah, Kindia, Dubréka and all *cercles* surrounding Conakry brought in rice, tubers and other food to feed the striking workers. It was in the course of this strike that Aïssata Mafory Bangoura emerged to become a leading figure among women P D G militants, exhorting Guinean woman to sell jewellery and clothes in order to help the strikers. Her meeting with Sékou Touré had changed her life. From that time onwards until her death in 1976, she became one of the P D G's staunchest supporters, leading anti-colonial demonstrations, and travelling through Guinea to the smallest villages to explain and discuss the party's policies.

The strike victory had a great impact throughout F W A, and particularly in Guinea where there was a 20 per cent wage rise and where the Labour Code was implemented according to the wishes of the Guinea trade union movement. It was a magnificent achievement for the P D G and trade unionists. According to the Labour Code, forced labour was abolished. The rights of trade unions were guaranteed. Workers were protected against sudden dismissal, and a 40-hour week with one full day of leisure was instituted. Further, there was to be equal pay for those doing the same work under the same conditions and with the same qualifications. There was to be an annual paid holiday, and legal protection against exploitation.

The link between economic exploitation and political domination had been clearly demonstrated. In 1953, almost half of urban wage earners in Guinea were employed in the public sector. In pressing therefore for economic improvement they were confronting the colonial administration both as employer and as foreign ruler. Cementing trade union and party cohesion was the election of labour leader Sékou Touré as member of the territorial assembly for Beyla in August 1953, his election giving the labour movement the necessary platform for political action.

During the nineteen-fifties, with the general disengagement of African political and quasi-political organizations from their French counterparts, Sékou Touré and his colleagues found links with French parties and trade unions hindered progress towards national liberation and economic improvement. They therefore took steps to Africanize the labour movement. In 1955, Sékou Touré, Seydou Diallo and Bassirou Guèye, all of whom were C G T secretaries, began a campaign to disaffiliate. At a R D A co-ordinating committee meeting in Conakry in July 1955, the question of the disaffiliation of African labour federations from French organizations was placed on the agenda. Some six months later, in January 1956, the Confédération Générale des Travailleurs Africains (C G T A) was created the membership coming largely from the C G T and F O. In July 1956, the Catholic C F T C followed suit by transforming itself into the Confédération Africaine des Travailleurs Croyants (C A T C). The African content of the labour movement had been established, but the need remained to unify. This was the objective of a congress held in Conakry in October 1956, when an agreement was signed by Sékou Touré on behalf of C G T A; Abdoulaye Diallo for C G T; and David Soumah for C A T C. At a follow-up conference held in Cotonou in January 1957, the first African labour confederation was created, the Union Générale des Travailleurs d'Afrique Noire (U G T A N). This was largely the work of Sékou Touré who became the U G T A N's first secretary-general. From that moment, Guinean trade unionism assumed an entirely political form. Sékou Touré was not only secretary-general of U G T A N but was also vice-president of the Territorial Assembly as leader of the P D G. Henceforth, P D G and labour movement were one and the same. This was affirmed during the first congress of U G T A N cadres held in Bamako in March 1958. Sékou Touré advocated a single labour movement dominated by the party, and this was accepted.

Unlike contemporary national figures in, for example, Ivory Coast and Senegal, who had gained their political experience within the French administration, Sékou Touré had emerged through the trade union movement and through the P D G. His reputation as a dynamic party and labour leader was high throughout F W A. He was known for his radical policies and for his Africanism. He was the antithesis of the 'francophone man'.

Alarmed by the turn of events in Africa, the French government sought to placate national fervour by increasing economic 'aid' to the colonies through F I D E S. Whereas the first ten-year development plan had concentrated on building the economic infrastructure of roads, ports, airports, schools, hospitals and so on, in 1953 a second plan, emphazised industrial and agricultural development. The labour leader, Sékou Touré then only thirty-one years old, had already become the dominant personality not only in the P D G–R D A but in inter-territorial politics and in the trade union movement. Membership of the C G T in Guinea rose from 2,600 in 1953 to 10,700 in 1954, and to 39,000 in 1955 the year in which Sékou Touré became mayor of Conakry.

Sékou Touré was elected to the Guinea Territorial Assembly in 1953. But in the following year, he was declared to be the loser in a by-election to fill the vacancy of deputy in the French Assembly caused by the death of Yacine Diallo. Sékou Touré, who had travelled constantly throughout

Guinea and enjoyed the enthusiastic support of people in every region except possibly the Fouta Djallon, campaigned against privileged groups in Guinean society, and denounced the luxurious way of life of deputies. He was opposed by a new party formed by various ethnic and regional groups, the *Bloc Africain de Guinée* (B A G), their candidate being Barry Diawadou, a Fula who came from a chiefly family and was an ex-pupil of the École Normale William Ponty. A third candidate was Barry Ibrahima, known as Barry III of the *Démocratie Socialiste de Guinée* (D S G). According to the official result, Diawadou, who was supported by the Gaullists and the colonial administration, obtained 147,701 votes, Sékou Touré 85,906, and Barry III 7,995. This obviously rigged result which the P D G–R D A refused to accept, was followed by demonstrations in many parts of Guinea. They were sternly suppressed by the French. In areas where support for Sékou Touré was known to be strong, P D G voters had been struck off the voting roll, and P D G ballot papers were not distributed. Even the French socialist party (S F I O) condemned the dishonest ways in which the election had been conducted, and called for the recall of Governor Parisot. So great was the reaction to the election rigging both in Guinea and France that the Minister of T O M, Robert Buron, was compelled to visit Guinea in October 1954 and to promise fair elections in future. He made a particular point of showing courtesy towards Sékou Touré and other leading members of the P D G.

There followed within the next six months developments which gave the French government a new sense of urgency in its handling of colonial problems. The situation in Indo-China was deteriorating. Dien Bien Phu fell in May 1954. In North Africa, the Algerian war of independence broke out in November necessitating the declaration of a state of emergency in April 1955. The same month, the Afro-Asian Bandung Conference took place at which four sub-Saharan states were represented. They were Ethiopia, Liberia, the Gold Coast and Sudan. France forbade the representation of Tunisia, Algeria and Morocco, but an unofficial North African delegation representing the nationalist parties of all three countries was present. The conference condemned French policy in North Africa and called for the independence of all colonial peoples. It was the first time that Africans and Asians had sat down together in conference and agreed on a common strategy to end colonialism. The French government took note and realized the dramatic effect the Bandung manifesto would have on colonized people thoughout the world. Clearly, France had to try to find an acceptable alternative to independence if the French Union was to survive.

In the nineteen-fifties there had been significant advances towards independence in British colonies in West Africa. A breakthrough had been achieved in the Gold Coast where the Convention People's Party (C P P) led by Kwame Nkrumah was campaigning for 'self-government *now*'. On 10 July 1953, Nkrumah in the famous Motion of Destiny speech in the National Assembly in Accra called on Britain to fix a firm date for independence. He had become prime minister in March 1952, and the Gold Coast was well on the way to becoming the first African colony to win independence. In Nigeria, there were also African cabinet ministers as the country progressed towards independence.

Although these developments were eagerly noted among French-speaking Africans, the backward-looking such as Boigny and Senghor, continued to assert that African states needed the protection of France. 'We consider ourselves better off than our comrades in the Gold Coast, in Liberia or British Gambia,' Senghor declared. Many in F W A agreed with him, that integration with France was still the best solution provided there was some increase in territorial power. But there were a growing number who, like Sékou Touré, envisaged a time when the African peoples of F W A would govern themselves even if links with France were not entirely severed.

In the elections of 1956, which were on the whole free from large scale interference, the R D A re-emerged as the largest African party with nine deputies. Among them were Modibo Keita of Soudan, Sékou Touré and Diallo Saifoulaye both of Guinea. Sékou Touré's vote had increased by over 250,000 since the 1954 by-election. As far as the results in France were concerned, there was a marked swing back towards the Left. The Gaullists lost heavily, and Guy Mollet the socialist leader became prime minister in a Left-centre coalition. Boigny was appointed a *ministre-délégué* in the prime-minister's office. One of the first measures to be passed in the Assembly was an amnesty for all R D A supporters in prison or deprived of their political rights. For the French government was prepared to contemplate major constitutional reform to avoid if possible any further spread of armed struggle in the colonies.

It was felt in France that it would be easier to deal separately with each of the eight colonies and the mandated territory of Togo than with a federation representing a total population of some thirty million. A weakening of the federal government also suited Ivory Coast, which was making economic progress far beyond the other territories, and which resented having to support the less prosperous areas of F W A. Most federal organizations at some time or another face this problem. The richer feel they should not be expected to bolster up the poorer indefinitely. Senghor and the I O M on the other hand, opposed any lessening of federal power because it would balkanize and therefore weaken the voice of Africans within the French Union.

As the territories tended to develop along separate lines, the R D A split up into national parts, and so also did the I O M. Soon, there was no party which spread across all territories in the federation. Crisis point was reached in the R D A conference of 1957 when differences among the leadership became clear. It was at his conference that Sékou Touré and Modibo Keita emerged to present a serious challenge to the domination of Senghor and Boigny. Both Sékou Touré and Modibo Keita supported a strong, independent federation which would maintain close links with France. Boigny on the other hand, wanted each territory to govern itself, maintaining individual links with France and remaining in the French Union.

Splits within the R D A were not new. Ever since 1950, Boigny had been criticized for being too cooperative with

France. Branches of the R D A in Senegal, Niger and Cameroon had failed to follow him and had been expelled from the organization. Trade unions had also criticized Boigny's position in the French cabinet, and his agreement to support the use of West African troops on the French side in the Algerian war of liberation. Among those who were extremely critical of Boigny and his policies was Sékou Touré who was rapidly becoming the most radical of African leaders in F W A.

Sékou Touré, unlike Boigny, Senghor, Apithy and most other African deputies in the French Assembly, spent much more of his time in Africa than in Paris. But he did attend debates on the Loi Cadre. The main issues were the questions of how much power should be given to the Territorial Assemblies, and what was to be the composition of the new Councils of Government. According to the draft proposal, the Council of Government was to be presided over by the colonial governor, and to be nominated by him. It was not, therefore, to be responsible to the Territorial Assembly, an arrangement which would leave the latter in a very weak position. All the most important matters were to be classed as *services d'état* (state powers), to be administered directly from Paris.

An amendment submitted by Apithy proposed that the territories should have real internal autonomy, each territory having its own prime minister elected by the Territorial Assembly. The prime minister would nominate other members of the Council of Government, which would be collectively responsible to the legislature. Key matters such as education, law and order, labour relations and trade should be classed as *services territoriaux* (territorial powers) and not *services d'état*. These proposals were supported by the P C F and other radical members of the Assembly including Sékou Touré who represented the R DA. Apithy duly presented them to the National Assembly in the name of the T O M Commission on 29 January 1957.

Some of Apithy's proposals were adopted, but there were no significant concessions on the powers of Territorial Assemblies. The governor of each territory was still to preside over its executive council, though all remaining members were to be elected by the Assemblies. The vice-president of the Council of Government would be the prime minister in all but name. But the French Assembly would not agree to the transference of important powers from the list of state powers to that of territorial powers. State powers reserved to the French government were defence, foreign affairs, currency and economic development financed by F I D E S. The Territorial Assemblies, which were to be elected on a basis of universal suffrage, were to control agriculture, health, primary and secondary education (except syllabuses and exams), internal trade and the domestic civil service.

In March 1957, elections were held throughout F W A under the Loi Cadre. These were the first elections where there was a single voters' roll and universal suffrage. The R D A won outright control of the Assemblies in Ivory Coast, Soudan (now Mali) and Guinea. In Upper Volta, the R D A was the senior partner in a coalition government. In A E F, the R D A was also the largest single party, its strength being mainly in Chad.

During April and May the new Assemblies elected the Territorial Councils of Government, and for the first time, African party leaders began to assume executive responsibilities in their own countries. R D A members controlled about half of the Great Councils of A O F and A E F. Sékou Touré became vice-president in Guinea where the R D A won all but four of the seats. In Soudan, Modibo Keita emerged victorious but preferred not to occupy the office of vice-president. In Upper Volta and Gabon, R D'A leaders became heads of coalition governments.

The victories of R D A throughout F W A, enhanced the position of Sékou Touré and Modibo Keita, and heralded a decline in the pre-eminence of Boigny. This represented a fundamental shift in attitude among Africans away from France and towards Africa. In this connection, an interesting event occured in April 1957 when Nkrumah, prime minister of newly-independent Ghana, visited Ivory Coast and met Boigny, then a minister in the French government. At an official reception in Abidjan's parliament building on the last night of Nkrumah's stay, Boigny said that he saw great virtue in a system which enabled a leader in West Africa, such as himself, to have experience as a minister in the metropolitan country. 'You are witnessing the start of two experiements', he said. 'A wager has been made between two territories, one having chosen independence, the other preferring the difficult road to the construction, with the metropole of a community of men equal in rights and duties.'[13] Nkrumah replied that Ghana had chosen the only possible way to real freedom, and that the 'independence' of his friends in A O F would prove illusory. Freedom and independence came first; equality and fraternity afterwards.

Evidently, Boigny had accepted the 'toys and lollipops' offered by the French government. So also, it appeared had many of the officials and administrators who held power as a result of the recent elections. Five of the twelve new vice-presidents of the Councils of Government, and both the new presidents of the Great Councils were men with French parliamentary experience. In addition, there were in all the Councils of Government, European Frenchmen chosen by African leaders to assist in the work of government.

It was just after his visit to Ivory Coast in April 1957, that Nkrumah and Sékou Touré first met. Nkrumah went on to Guinea from Abidjan. At that time, the Guinean P D G leader was generally considered to have a political outlook much closer to Nkrumah than to Boigny. It was noted by newsmen that Nkrumah and Sékou Touré 'seemed to take to each other on first sight; both believe in Pan Africa'.[14] Nkrumah spent a week in Guinea, and they discussed 'many common problems'. At the end of the visit, Sékou Touré accepted an invitation to go to Ghana to see 'independence in action'.

Controversy continued in F W A over the federal issue between those, like Sékou Touré and Modibo Keita, who thought federal executives were needed in Dakar and Brazzaville, and those who supported Boigny in advocating territorial autonomy, each territory making its own arrangements direct with France. At the R D A conference held in Bamako in September 1957, Boigny declared that the Franco-African Community was already a reality. At that time, Sékou Touré was also in favour of a Community based on equality, but he wanted elected federal governments for A O F and A E F to enable Africans to manage their own affairs, and to provide a powerful African voice within the Community. If each territory was a separate entity and there was no independent federal government, their bargaining position with the French government would be extremely weak. While Boigny considered it more effective to exert pressure from within, through a political group in Paris, Sékou Touré preferred to be a minister in a West African government in Dakar.

After much discussion in Bamako, a compromise formula was worked out, and reluctantly accepted by Sékou Touré:

> Conscious of the indissoluble economic, political and cultural bonds which unite the territories, and anxious to preserve the destinies of the African Community, the Congress instructs its elected representatives to put down a Bill tending to democratize the existing federal executive organs.

Boigny emerged from the conference with his position in F W A very lowered. Apart from his obvious support for the French line, he had offended African opinion by his attitude towards the Front de Libération Nationale (F L N), the Algerian national movement. Boigny was prepared to advise them to end the armed struggle and to join the Franco-African Community. Sékou Touré, however, declared that the R D A should call on the French government to 'negotiate with the authentic representatives of the Algerian people'. The Congress went on to elect a new Coordination Committee. Boigny continued as president, but Sékou Touré, Modibo Keita and Gabriel Lisette (Chad) became vice-presidents.

When he returned to Conakry, Sékou Touré reaffirmed the view of the P D G–R D A that the Great Council of A O F should be transformed into a federal assembly which would then elect an executive responsible for all the common services of the member territories. Inherent in this stand was the gradual moving of Guinea towards total rejection of the Franco-African Community.

5

'NON'

In West Africa, the national liberation movements of British colonies concentrated mainly on non-violent methods of struggle since this proved to be the most effective procedure. There was 'positive action' in the form of strikes, boycotts, demonstrations and civil disobedience, but in general no call to arms. The British, accustomed to a two-party system with a strong executive, did not find too much difficulty in handling the decolonization process. Colonial protest, when it could not be contained, was met with a mixture of repression and grudging reform, until at length when it could no longer be denied, full self-government was granted. Replacing British colonial administrations were indigenous governments provided with the structure and traditions of British institutions.

Peoples of other colonial territories had to fight for their freedom. For example, the peoples of Algeria, Guinea Bissau, Mozambique and Angola waged a protracted guerrilla struggle to end colonial rule. As far as the French West African colonies were concerned, the policy of the French government was to bring them into as close a union with France as possible, and if this failed, to resort to the harsh suppression of nationalist movements. For the French government, it was a matter of national pride that France's colonies chose to remain French. Many years before other colonial powers stopped talking about 'colonies' and 'empire' the French spoke of 'territories' and 'union' or 'community'. While the British developed the 'Commonwealth', the French promoted the idea of 'Francophonie'. Guinea, which chose not to belong to the Franco-African Community, was deemed to have 'seceded', and was therefore recognized as independent. It was perhaps the strangest way for a colony to achieve its independence.

In Ivory Coast and Senegal, as in other former French colonies where there is a francophile leadership, the French government has virtually guaranteed the continuance of pro-French regimes through the presence of French troops and French advisers, and through the closest of economic ties. Even when at last the final trace of 300 years of French sovereignty in Africa disappeared with the independence of Djibouti on 26 June 1977, President Giscard d'Estaing of France announced that a treaty, two agreements and three conventions had been signed with the newly-independent state. It was agreed that 4,000 French troops should remain in Djibouti. Since the local forces only numbered some 2,000 men, the genuineness of Djibouti's independence was very much open to question. France has maintained strong links with most of its former colonies, with the notable exception of Guinea.

In Guinea, the French encountered a theory of independence, a quality of leadership, and a degree of political organization and militancy among the people which they did not know how to handle. Sékou Touré and the P D G rejected the idea that certain conditions such as political maturity and a stable government must exist before independence: 'All peoples', said Sékou Touré, 'are capable at any time of administering themselves and developing their personality. There are no minor peoples, except under slavery or foreign oppression.'[1] It was to be typical of Guinea that it was the first French West African colony to obtain independence, and that Guinea alone, of all the 'French' territories voted *'Non'* in de Gaulle's 1958 referendum for membership of the Franco-African Community.

During the months leading up to the referendum, Sékou Touré as vice-president of the Council was in effect prime minister of Guinea. The French governor, Jean Ramadier, was content to remain in the background and to allow Sékou Touré to preside at Council meetings, and to implement various reforms. Local government was reorganized. The villages of Guinea were transformed into 'rural communes' administered by councils of five to fifteen members elected for a five year term. Council presidents were named village chiefs. The twenty-five *cercles* were renamed *circonscriptions*. These became 'administrative regions' after independence, each being administered by officials appointed by the government. Some ninety-three administrative units, later named *arrondissements*, were formed as dependencies of the *circonscriptions*. The chiefs had been appendages of the colonial administration. They were salaried officials responsible for tax collection and the maintenance of law and order. It was part of P D G policy to abolish them.

The way in which the P D G brought about the abolition of chieftainship at that time is typical of the methodical way in which the party works, and it is worth examining in some detail how it was accomplished. A national conference was called to consider the question of chieftainship as a result of which political representatives were appointed in every canton to be responsible for taxes, thus weakening the position of canton chiefs. In addition, the party appointed magistrates for local courts in all *cercles*. Party militants were told, 'Don't go to the colonial judges any more, but deal with the indigenous tribunal; try your best to have all matters settled among us, Africans.'[2] The P D G went on to nominate 'assistants' to the colonial *cercle* commandant, though in law it had no power to do so. Indigenous provident societies were abolished and replaced by cooperatives whose leaders were elected by the peasants. 'In every sector, we trimmed the structures of the colonial power and substituted for them that which could confer active power on the people and on the organs of leadership.'[3]

Initially, only 'unjust' chiefs and the most unpopular ones were dismissed, their removal being greeted with 'applause' by the people. Every fortnight a list of dismissed chiefs was published until by December 1957, chieftainship had been abolished, and with it the main bulwark of French colonial power at local level. The whole process had taken only six months and had been accomplished with the full support and understanding of the people at every stage.

There was an immediate outcry in Paris, not only in

government circles but among Guinean students. The latter sent a resolution to the P D G stating that chieftainship was an essential part of African society and a 'stabilizing' force. In the words of Sékou Touré, 'the youths did not understand anything of the situation and the colonial regime merely used them as a smoke screen'.[4] The colonial authorities went on to summon all A O F, Togo and Malagasy government vice-presidents to a meeting in Paris to discuss the abolition of chieftainship in Guinea. The meeting was addressed by one of the vice-presidents, whom Sékou Touré does not name, but whom he says was 'prepared' by the French government. The member declared: 'My Guinean brothers, you must understand that France alone was responsible for the freedom of our countries. France our motherland could not tolerate illegal measures. It is a country of order, justice, fraternity and democracy. Chieftainship is not a disorder. Neither is it arbitrary. You want to deprive our society of its original basis.' Sékou Touré, exasperated by the 'senseless verbiage', rose to reply. He began: 'We sincerely pity Africa for having brought forth sons of the category of that nameless, worthless man who has no dignity and no freedom, and who now speaks of the civilizing mission of his French fatherland.'[5] The rest of the speech Sékou Touré says he will not repeat, but the tone can be imagined. Listening, were representatives of all the semi-autonomous governments of A O F and also the French minister for the colonies. Needless to say, the colonialists did not publish the minutes of the conference.

There was no going back. Chieftainship has been abolished in Guinea and the way was opened for the transition towards the adaption of the colony to the imperatives of a democratic and progressive state. 'This was the party's move towards national independence, which made of the party through the multiple adjustments of its organization, of its working methods, the party of the democratic revolution.'[6] When elections were held in May 1958 for the *conseils de circonscriptions*, the P D G gained over 87 per cent of all votes cast. This result was to prove a very significant factor in Guinea's 'No' vote in the subsequent referendum. For in other territories, the chiefs gave their support to the constitution, and urged their peoples to do likewise.

Along with local government reform, measures were taken to Africanize the civil service, and to extend social security benefits to those, such as day labourers, who had previously not been eligible for them. Family allowances were increased. Secondary education was expanded, and a School of Administration founded. In the meantime, with the collapse of the French government in May 1958, and the return of General de Gaulle to power, a reorganization of the relationship between France and her overseas territories became a matter of top priority. A committee was set up to consider the drafting of a constitution for the Fifth Republic. The basic question at issue was whether the individual territories of A O F and A E F should be linked with France in a community, or whether autonomous federations of A O F and A E F should be formed and linked with France.

At the Conakry congress of the P D G held in June 1958, a resolution was passed calling for the foundation of autonomous states in A O F and A E F, each with a legislative assembly and an executive; and a federal state which the autonomous states, plus France and other states of the French Union would join. The federation would have a common parliament and executive with responsibility for foreign affairs, defence, overall economic policy, currency, justice and higher education. Sékou Touré declared that the existing Great Councils must be transformed into legislative assemblies, and that A O F and A E F must have responsible federal executives to take over the work of the French High Commissioners, and the French Overseas Ministry. Under such an arrangement, overseas France would no longer be represented in the French National Assembly or in the metropolitan cabinet, but only in federal institutions. Sékou Touré wanted to see the Assemblée de l'Union Française transformed into the new federal parliament.

While the debate for and against federal executives was being argued in Africa, African deputies in Paris were regrouping in an attempt to present a united front. Representing the R D A were Sékou Touré, Modibo Keita, Abdoulaye

Diallo and d' Arboussier, none of whom supported Boigny's views. A minimum political programme was drawn up stipulating complete internal autonomy for the territories of A O F and A E F, and a federal republic joining France to the groups of territories and the ungrouped territories on a basis of free cooperation, absolute equality and the right to independence. The government of the federal republic would retain control of foreign affairs, defence, currency, higher education and the judiciary. The various parties were to unite on this basis, the majority party in each territory absorbing the others, but adopting a new name. The latter provision caused difficulty because the R D A refused to give up its name.

Although Sékou Touré's campaign for federal executives, and a united African party appeared to gain widespread support, the meeting of the R D A coordination committee in Ivory Coast on 10 March failed to reach any decision. The split continued among those who supported the Sékou Touré line, and those like Boigny who wished to see each territory making its own arrangements with France. At the Regroupment Congress held in Dakar on 26 March 1958, the R D A again refused to give up its name, and R D A opponents founded a new party called the Parti du Regroupement Africain (P R A). Founding this party were the Convention Africain led by Senghor, the French African Socialist Party (M S A) led by Lamine Guèye, and five smaller parties including the Rassemblement Démocratique Voltaique headed by Gerard Ouedrago, and the Rassemblement Démocratique Dahoméen, led by Hubert Maga. The R D A, however, agreed to form a common front with the P R A and any other party which wished to join them on a programme of 'African action'. The objective of this action was to be complete internal autonomy for each of the territories of A O F and A E F; the grouping of these territories into two federations to whose governments the territories would yield certain powers; the federal governments to be responsible to federal assemblies, to have internal sovereignty and the right to opt for independence.

When, therefore, the A O F Great Council met on 27

March 1958, Sékou Touré proposed that A O F should function for the time being on a two party parliamentary system since it was not possible to form a single united party. A resolution was passed calling for a representative and responsible federal executive to direct the subjects allocated to the federal government by the eight territories of A O F. At that time, these subjects were under the direction of the French High Commissioner and his staff. Members of the Great Council could scrutinize and comment on the High Commissioner's activities, but could not issue directions or initiate legislation. The resolution went on to urge the granting of full internal autonomy for the territories as an indispensable corollary to the setting up of a federal executive.

When in July 1958, a committee was set up to consider the drafting of a constitution for the Fifth Republic, both the R D A and the P R A submitted proposals. The P R A wanted a federal republic composed of separate republics which would delegate to it certain legislative powers. The federal president, de Gaulle, would be the central executive, but the federal assembly would be merely a forum in which members from overseas and from metropolitan France could meet and discuss matters of common interest. The R D A on the other hand, wanted a federal parliament to which the federal government would be responsible. But in spite of their differences, the P R A and R D A issued a joint declaration on 18 July 1958 insisting on the recognition of the right to independence.

In view of the political climate of the time they could not do otherwise. Ghana's independence in 1957 had sparked off a chain reaction throughout Africa, and it would have been political suicide for any African leader not to declare in favour of self-government. Similarly, it was necessary to pay at least lip service to the idea of African unity. In April 1958, Nkrumah reactivated panafricanism on the soil of Africa when he summoned the first Conference of Independent African States to meet in Accra. There were then only eight independent states.[7] Eight months later, in December 1958, Nkrumah called the first All-African Peoples' Conference. This conference, attended by freedom fighters, members of nationalist parties, trade unionists, representatives of cooperative and youth movements from all over Africa, further stimulated panafricanism and the drive towards the total liberation of the African continent from foreign domination.

The West African colonies of France were particularly susceptible to the wind of change blowing strongly from their near neighbour, Ghana. In Senegal, Senghor's statement that 'independence has no positive content, it is not a solution', was challenged by the Union Progressiste Sénégalaise, the Senegalese section of the P R A, Lamine-Guèye declaring: 'I am for independence without conditions.' Bakary Djibo of Niger at the P R A founding congress held in Cotonon 25–27 July 1958, stated: 'You can only associate when you're already independent. National independence first, the rest later.' Emile Derlin Zinsou, usually a supporter of close association with France, expressed the view that the territories must be free to link with other states, and even to withdraw from the French community. Bass Madiop of Soudan went further: 'Up to now,' he said, 'we have called on France, but now we shall have to call on ourselves.' A telegram sent by Boigny, in which he expressed the hope that the Cotonou Congress would 'bring realistic elements construction Franco-African Community' was greeted with derisive laughter.

Delegates went on to pass a resolution rejecting de Gaulle's draft constitution and calling for a constituent assembly of Afrique Noire to negotiate for a multinational confederation of free and equal peoples, without abandoning the African will to federate into a United States of Africa. Congress then adopted the password of 'Independence Now'. Strangely, Senghor was largely responsible for drawing up the resolution, though when questioned by a journalist on whether he really intended to implement 'Indépendance Now', he with typical ambiguity replied: 'L'Indépendance immédiate, certes oui, mais non pas dans l'immédiat.' Meanwhile, in Paris, the French government transferred all powers still exercised by the governors and presidents of the cabinets of the overseas territories to their African vice-presidents creating in effect African prime ministers.

When the Consultative Constitutional Committee was set up in Paris to consider the new constitution, Senghor and Lamine-Guèye representing the P R A, Lisette the R D A, and Philibert Tsiranana head of the government of Madagascar, were the African members of the Committee. Sékou Touré went to Paris, and was chosen by the R D A to see de Gaulle on their behalf. But he was not a member of the Committee, and it was therefore Boigny's policy, expressed through Lisette, rather than those of the majority of R D A which was put forward. As the discussions proceeded, and the arguments for and against federal executives were put, de Gaulle lost patience. 'Of course I understand the attractions of independence and the lure of secession,' he told the Committee, 'the referendum will tell us whether secession carries the day. But what is inconceivable is an independent state which France continues to help. If the choice is for independence, the government will draw, with regret, the conclusions that follow from the expression of that choice.' In other words, independence and membership of the Community was not a choice open to Africans. If they voted 'Yes' in the referendum they would commit themselves to no independence. For de Gaulle rejected the idea of a confederation consisting of independent states, and insisted on a federation the members of which would cede part of their sovereignty to the federal government. The Community would have a president, an executive council, a senate and a court of appeal. The French president, elected by an electoral college in which overseas members would be a small minority, would automatically be president of the Community. The executive council would consist of the president, the prime ministers of the French Republic and overseas member states; and the ministers responsible for foreign policy, defence, currency, overall economic policy, strategic raw materials, justice, higher education and communications – all of which would be dealt with by the Community government. The senate would consist of delegates chosen by the parliaments of member states in proportion to their populations.

The draft constitution of the Fifth Republic was published on 30 July 1958, and it was then announced that a referendum would be held on it in September. Once the constitution had been accepted, there was to be no more question of self-determination, still less of the right to independence. The option favoured by Sékou Touré of an autonomous federal executive was not to be given. The overseas peoples were to accept or reject the Franco-African Community. Any territory rejecting the Community would automatically become independent and deprived of French economic aid. It was a case of 'take it or leave it'.

Sékou Touré and those who opposed the constitution, considered that it gave far too much power to the Community government. If the key areas of foreign policy, economic affairs and justice were outside the control of local assemblies how could there be genuine autonomy of the overseas territories? Quite clearly there was to be no *equal* partnership.

The referendum was due to take place on 28 September 1958. But before then, de Gaulle was to visit each of the 'French' territories in Africa to explain the constitutional proposals. The French government's final version of the proposed constitution would not be made known until after his return, though it was widely believed that the French cabinet had accepted the main changes proposed by the Consultative Constitutional Committee. These were, that overseas territories should have the choice of maintaining their present position, becoming a French overseas department, or joining a French Community. The Community would have a legislature and a cabinet consisting of prime ministers of member states and of the ministers concerned with the subjects within the Community's competence. Each member of the Community would have full internal autonomy; and they could if they wished group themselves into primary federations. In addition, at the end of five years, an overseas territory could choose to become independent.

When de Gaulle set out on his African trip in August 1958, it was well known that he considered a loose confederal relationship of the overseas territories with France as out of the question. In his view, there was no possible intermediate status. The territories had to choose between the Community, or total independence without any help from France. He went first to Madagascar. From there he flew to Brazzaville, where he was received with great enthusiasm. The people regarded him as a war hero, and the architect of the Brazzaville Conference of 1944. In a speech in Brazzaville, de Gaulle actually used the word 'independence' when he said that the overseas territories could not only choose independence by voting 'No' in the referendum, but could also later decide to leave the proposed federal community and become independent. Such assurances must have sounded strange to those who remembered the thousands of Vietnamese, Algerian and Malagasy patriots who had been killed by French troops for demanding their independence. From Brazzaville, de Gaulle went on to Ivory Coast. According to a reporter, 'delirium reached its height at Abidjan, M. Houphouët-Boigny's fief, where the cheering crowds were uncontrollable'.[8] He received a very different reception, however, when he arrived in Conakry on the 27th of August. Hostile crowds shouting independence slogans lined the streets from the airport. Sékou Touré, the leading supporter of federal executives in Dakar and Brazzaville, was determined that the General should be left in no doubt of the PDG's attitude to the referendum. He told de Gaulle that the right to independence must be written into the new constitution. But de Gaulle refused to go beyond the statement he made in Brazzaville, when he said that if a territory chose to become independent at some future date, France would 'raise no obstacles'. Sékou Touré had already taken up de Gaulle's indirect threat to withdraw French aid when he declared on 9 August: 'General de Gaulle has said that we can take independence with all its consequences. I shall reply, for my part, that the consequences are not exclusively African but may be French as well.' In Conakry, during de Gaulle's visit, Sékou Touré again informed the General that Guinea could not accept a constitution which did not specifically confirm the right to independence. The right to secede and to take the consequences was not good enough – though Guinea would do just that if necessary.

De Gaulle was unimpressed. He repeated his 'raise no obstacles' phrase: 'I say it here,' he declared in Conakry, 'even louder than elsewhere: independence is at Guinea's disposal. She can take it by saying "No" to the proposal which is made to her; and in that case I guarantee that metropolitan France will raise no obstacles. Naturally, she will draw the conclusions, but she will raise no obstacles.' The thinly-veiled threat to withdraw all economic aid was not missed by Sékou Touré. Speaking in the Territorial Assembly, with his back half-turned to de Gaulle, Sékou Touré strongly criticized French colonial policies, and it was then that he declared: 'We, for our part, have a first and indispensable need, that of our dignity. Now there is no freedom without dignity. We prefer poverty in freedom to riches in slavery.' He went on to speak of Africa's united and independent future.

Could the close resemblance between Sékou Touré's courageous words, and Nkrumah's well-known statement: 'We prefer self-government with danger to servitude in tranquillity,' be mere coincidence? Sékou Touré's speech visibly angered de Gaulle, and from this moment, the General regarded Guinea as lost. It was widely reported that he remarked to members of his entourage that Sékou Touré was 'a man we shall never get on with'. A dinner party planned for that evening with the Guinea government was promptly cancelled. So also was de Gaulle's invitation to Sékou Touré to accompany him when he flew to Dakar the following day.

On arrival in Senegal, de Gaulle again met unfriendly crowds chanting slogans such as 'Go away de Gaulle', and 'We want independence'. At a public meeting the next day, when the General was constantly interrupted, he shouted: 'Well, if you want independence then take it, on September 28.' The principal P R A leaders, were out of the country at the time of de Gaulle's visit, but other P R A leaders apologized to the General for the crowd's discourtesy, and blamed the demonstrations on the left-wing Parti de l'Indépendance Africain. Unlike Guinea, the leadership in Senegal was clearly unrepresentative of a united people.

At the end of de Gaulle's African tour it seemed likely that with the exception of Guinea, and possibly also of Niger, both P R A and R D A leaders in the ten remaining territories would advise their supporters to vote 'Yes' in the referendum. Those, however, who were associated with the U G T A N group of trade unions were committed to a 'No' vote. These included, apart from Sékou Touré and Bakary Djibo of Niger, Abdoulaye Guèye and Alioune Cisse of Senegal, and Abdoulaye Diallo of Soudan. These men met in Dakar after de Gaulle's departure and agreed to call for a 'No' vote subject to a cadre conference to be held in Bamako on 10 September. In a public statement made after the meeting, Sékou Touré declared:

> Between voting 'Yes' to a constitution which infringes the dignity, the unity and freedom of Africa, and accepting, as General de Gaulle says, immediate independence, Guinea will choose that independence without hesitating. We do not have to be blackmailed by France. We cannot yield on behalf of our countries to those who threaten and put pressure on us to make us choose, against heart and reason, the conditions of a marriage which would keep us within the complex of the colonial regime ... We say 'No' unanimously and categorically, to any project which does not cater for our aspirations.

How different was the attitude of Boigny who, on arriving in Paris on 26 August said: 'All territories will vote "Yes" ... Africans are not madmen.' It seems that he genuinely believed that Sékou Touré was bluffing, and that when the time came he would find a way to call for a 'Yes' vote after all.

On 11 September, the U G T A N cadre conference at Bamako decided to call for a 'No' vote. The following day, Sékou Touré declared that Guinea would vote 'No', and this decision was ratified by the P D G territorial conference two days later. 'We shall vote "No" to inequality, we shall vote "No" to irresponsibility. As from 29 September,' said Sékou Touré, 'we shall be an independent country.'

The final form of the proposed new French constitution did in fact incorporate the main changes put forward by the Constitutional Consultative Committee, and the text apparently satisfied most of the African peoples of A O F and A E F. When the referendum took place, on 28 September 1958, 95 per cent of the people of Guinea voted 'No'. Every other territory in A O F voted 'Yes'. In Senegal some 97 per cent of votes were in favour of the de Gaulle constitution; in Upper Volta, 91 per cent; in Ivory Coast, 99 per cent; in Niger 78 per cent. In A E F, all four territories returned a 'Yes' vote. The only political group which campaigned for a 'No' was the small Parti d'Union Nationale Gabonaise (P U N G A) in Gabon, consisting mainly of trade unionists and students.

The massive support for the constitution surprised many observers who expected more 'Noes' in Senegal, Niger and Dahomey where there was known to be opposition. In Senegal, three members of Mamadou Dia's P R A government had resigned in protest over the decision of the local section of the P R A to support the constitution. The Senegalese trade unions also opposed the constitution. But all the Muslim chiefs of Senegal urged the faithful to vote 'Yes'. In Niger, the P R A prime minister, Bakary Djibo, had campaigned for a 'No' vote. But he was opposed by several of his own ministers, by the chiefs, and by Hamani Diori's Niger R D A section. In Dahomey, P R A prime minister, Apithy, had encountered opposition from trade unionists.

Yet on the day of the referendum, the people as a whole, except for the Guineans, undoubtedly rallied to the call of their traditional leaders rather than to trade unionists and party leaders. The fact that the P D G had replaced the power of the chiefs by elected village councils in each of which the R D A had a majority, had much to do with the overwhelming 'No' vote in Guinea. But the decisive factor was the united stand of the P D G and the trade union movement. While the majority of people of the other A O F territories feared the consequences of a 'No' vote, Guineans were united in their determination to govern themselves, though it was ironic that a complete break with France was not envisaged by the people of Guinea until the weeks immediately preceding the referendum. Until then, they supported the plan for federal executives and the continuation of links with France. It was only when it became clear that this option was not open to them that Guineans prepared to face a future without France rather than agree to a Community in which they were convinced there would be no true freedom and equality.

The issues at stake in the referendum had been made clear to Guineans through many months of political campaigning by the P D G and through the trade union movement. At the U G T A N conference in Bamako in March 1958, attended by Sékou Touré, members had reaffirmed that trade unions must continue to play an important part in politics; and that U G T A N was in favour of territorial autonomy and federal executives, and advocated a 'No' vote in the referendum. This was precisely the view held by Sékou Touré. He was convinced of the need for federation within Africa. For he considered it the height of folly to divide 'French' Africa into separate states whose boundaries bore no relation to economic, social or cultural divisions.

Far from fearing the prospect of being dependent on themselves and on their own resources, the people of Guinea welcomed the challenge. As de Gaulle and his entourage discovered when they visted Guinea, Sékou Touré represented a unified and determined people. The ruling party, the P D G, was the party of the masses. It was no coincidence that its leadership had gained political experience through the African trade union movement, and not through elitist French organizations and the Paris legislature, like so many of the leaders in other territories of AOF and AEF.

On the very day on which the referendum results were declared, a French government official arrived in Conakry to inform Sékou Touré that Guinea was held to have seceded from France, and that there would be no more French economic aid. All French officials, numbering some 3,000 would be withdrawn within two months. The manner of Guinea's independence was both dramatic and unprecedented. In their haste to leave, the French took what they could with them and destroyed what they could not carry. Government records and files were torn up or burned; offices were stripped of their furniture and telephones. Even electric light bulbs and the handles on doors were removed. French administrators, doctors, teachers, engineers and businessmen flocked out of Guinea leaving virtually no trained replacements. Only 150 French government employees remained in Guinea, and 110 of these were teachers who chose to stay as volunteers. All French army units were withdrawn, including army doctors who took their medical supplies with them. French members of the police force left after first smashing the windows and furniture of their barracks. Guinean students in Paris and Dakar were stripped of their scholarships. French public investment in Guinea ceased, and the French government tried to stop private firms from investing there. When, at the end of November 1958, Sékou Touré moved into the former Governor's house in Conakry, he found that all the furniture and pictures had been removed, the cellars emptied, and the crockery smashed. Even the telephone had been ripped out.

De Gaulle clearly thought that Guinea would not be able to manage without French help; and it was the secret hope of many reactionaries in other countries, that independence in Guinea would be a failure. In France and elsewhere in the West, a press campaign began, except in the newspapers of the Left to discredit the P D G government. The French press was particularly hostile. It predicted chaos, and Guinea's incorporation into the eastern bloc. The following extract from *Figaro*, 29 September 1958, was typical:

> Mr Sékou Touré in calling for a vote of 'No' has completely unmasked himself. He has been for more than ten years a pawn which the Soviet machine has thrust into the political complex of Africa ... Mr Sékou Touré's role, clandestine until a few weeks ago, today consists in making Guinea into an agitator state in the heart of black Africa, for the benefit of the Soviet machine.

It was all part of what Sékou Touré described as the 'permanent plot' against the P D G government, which began among reactionary forces as soon as Guinea became independent. A newly-independent state could not have had a more difficult situation to handle than faced the people of Guinea after their courageous 'No' vote.

Sékou Touré did not underestimate the difficulties which lay ahead. He declared that Guinea would not celebrate independence since the country was entering a period not of 'dancing and rejoicing', but of 'war and austerity'. He knew he could depend on the support of the people. They had suffered much under colonialism, and were well prepared for further sacrifice. But they would suffer in order to build their country as a sovereign independent state. As Sékou Touré said: 'No sacrifice is too great for the man who is defending the liberty of his country.'

The Republic of Guinea was proclaimed on 2 October 1958, and the Territorial Assembly then transformed itself into a constituent assembly to draw up a new constitution. Sékou Touré was elected prime minister, and was also minister for foreign affairs and defence. It was a national government which included two members of the small PRA opposition and a former member of the Soudan government, Diallo Abdoulaye, who had been dismissed for campaigning for a 'No' vote in the referendum. There were eleven ministers and five secretaries of state in the cabinet. All ministers in the old cabinet kept their positions. Drame Alioune remained finance minister, Keita Fodeba kept his post as minister of the interior, and Mignard continued as minister of production. The two opposition leaders were Ibrahima Barry and Diawadou Barry III.

Guinea was the Second West African country to achieve independence, Ghana being the first. Significantly, Ghana was the first state to recognize the new government of Guinea, and Nkrumah further assisted Guinea by sponsoring its membership of the United Nations Organization (UNO).[9] The USSR, China, Egypt, Ethiopia, Morocco, Tunisia and Sudan enthusiastically welcomed the new state, and messages of goodwill were sent by Dr Azikiwe of Nigeria, Apithy of Dahomey, President Tubman of Liberia, Marshall Tito, and many others. Within three months, nine eastern bloc countries had signed bilateral agreements with Guinea, and Ghana had granted a loan of £10 million.[9] But although Sékou Touré wrote to many governments, including the United Kingdom, to seek recognition, most of them decided to await clarification from the French government as to the legal position of its former colony.

Almost overnight, Guinea had inspired the admiration of even her sternest critics. An observer declared that it was as if a large rock had been thrown into the colonial pond, causing the most profound repercussions. 'Whether he admits it or not; whether he is clearly or confusedly conscious of it, every African, every colonized person is concerned with the Guinea decision.'[10] Speaking at the Cinema Vox in Conakry on 2 October 1958, Sékou Touré's words were indeed prophetic: 'If they say in the Ivory Coast, in the Soudan or in Senegal that Guinea is lost because she chose liberty, then let them say it. I promise you that within two months we shall be showing the others the way.' By the end of 1960, every one of the former French colonies in A O F and A E F had followed Guinea's path and become independent, though in most cases it amounted to little more than 'flag independence'.

6

PDG POLICIES AND STRUCTURES

Guinea had achieved independence through a popular vote, and without preconditions. It might have seemed a promising base on which to build a newly-independent state. But the French had withdrawn leaving the people of Guinea almost completely unprepared. In addition to the usual conditions of under-development left behind by colonial powers when they surrendered direct political rule, Guinea was faced with the short-term problems of sheer survival. Not only were there major economic difficulties, but all the problems of temporary political isolation. Guineans found themselves cut off from the close political and economic associations established over many years as an overseas territory of France and a member of A O F. From a position of dependence, they had to make a rapid and complete change to self-reliance. Yet Guinea was without sufficient trained administrators and skilled personnel. Guinea had at most only half a dozen university graduates, and not one of them had occupied a responsible position in the colonial administration. The economy was a typically colonial one, geared to the needs of the colonial power. Financially, Guinea had a large budget deficit and was without capital reserves. About 60 per cent of Guinea's exports, at that time mainly bananas, went to France and had benefited from the lower customs duties by which France protected products from countries within the French Community. It was doubtful whether the French would allow this arrangement, and Guinea's membership of the franc monetary zone, to continue long enough to enable Guinea to adjust to the new situation and to form fresh trading patterns.

In common with other French overseas territories, public

development projects in Guinea had been paid for by France, and staffed mainly by officials paid by France. Although the French government retreated from its original position of recalling all French officials and technicians within two or three months, most of them were worried about their prospects in Guinea and were unwilling to stay unless offered very much higher salaries. Guinea was anxious to keep the services of teachers, doctors and technicians, but not administrators. French local officials, like the *chefs des circonscriptions* and police officers, had already been replaced by Guineans. The judiciary, however, was short of qualified Guineans to take over from French lawyers. The minister of justice, Camara Damatang, was compelled to consider sending for senior Guinean law students studying in France to fill posts in the magistracy. Fortunately, such emergency measures gradually became unnecessary as qualified professional and technical personnel from many parts of Africa, inspired by Guinea's example, applied to work in Guinea. Among the first to be recruited was Diallo Abdoulaye, the former minister of labour in Soudan. Others, not only from Africa, but from progressive movements throughout the world soon followed as countries particularly from the eastern bloc hastened to recognize the new state and to make economic agreements.

Also on the credit side, Guinea was rich in scarcely-tapped natural resources. With expanded agricultural production, the country could become self-sufficient in food. Equally important, there were large mineral resources, the development of which depended on overseas investment. Guinea already exported diamonds, iron ore and bauxite. Schemes to develop hydro-electric power, and to convert bauxite into alumina and aluminium, and iron ore into steel, were already attracting the interest of businessmen far beyond the hitherto narrow confines of the French Community. The hydro-electric scheme involving a dam to be built on the Konkouré River, and an aluminium factory to be built at Souapite by the internationally financed company of F R I A, was fundamental to plans to industrialize Guinea. It was to be paid for partly by a long-term loan from France, and partly by another larger loan from international sources on the guarantee of France. Guinea's independence raised a big question mark over the future of the Konkouré dam, though the Guinean minister of commerce declared that his country was determined to go ahead with industrialization and that Guinea would gurantee the loan from the International Bank. Sékou Touré endorsed the statement, saying that Guineans would, if necessary build the dam with their own hands: 'What else,' he said, 'is the dam, but earth, and we have plenty of earth?'[1]

But perhaps the greatest long-term asset which Guinea had at independence, apart from her economic potential and the support of progressive forces throughout the world, was the high degree of political organization of the people, manifested in the P D G, and led so ably by Sékou Touré. 'For any organized people,' said Sékou Touré, 'every problem has its just radical solution.' Guineans had, by the popular 'No' vote of 1958, participated en masse in the attainment of independence. This was to be the prelude for full people's participation in the building of the independent state of Guinea. Members of the B A G and M S A were incorporated into the P D G and their leaders became ministers in the new Guinean government. Sékou Touré uses the term 'communocracy', meaning that the state is administered through the active cooperation of everyone. The individual is merged in the state which he has helped to build, and in which he achieves his highest fulfilment. An eminent member of the American Communist Party, visiting Guinea shortly after independence, wrote that 'popular energies are liberated, the participation of the masses is effective and permanent at every level'.[2] According to Sékou Touré: 'Decolonization does not consist merely in liberating oneself from the presence of colonialism. It must necessarily be completed in the total liberation of the spirit of the colonized.'[3] He went on: 'Our unceasing efforts will be directed towards finding our own ways of development, if we wish our evolution and our emancipation to take place without our personality being thereby altered. Every time we adopt a solution authentically African in its nature and conception, we shall solve our problems easily because all who take part in it will be neither disorientated nor surprised by what they have to achieve.'[4]

The few so-called intellectuals in Guinea at independence expected to become the new administrators, ambassadors, directors of hospitals and schools. But the P D G was unimpressed by their degrees and diplomas. What counted was their degree of commitment to the service of the people. The ancestors of the people of Guinea had built and administered vast empires without a French education. It was thanks to the people that Guinea had achieved independence. Therefore, only genuine militants, the politically educated, were appointed regardless of academic qualifications.

The constitution of the Republic of Guinea, adopted on 10 November 1958, proclaimed the 'equality and solidarity of all its citizens without distinction as to race, sex or creed'. Guinea was to be a republic 'based on the principles of democracy, freedom of religion and social justice'. The national anthem was entitled *Liberty* and the motto of the republic was declared to be: 'Work, Justice, Solidarity.' National sovereignty was to reside in the people 'who shall exercise it in all matters through their deputies to the National Assembly' which alone should pass laws. Its members were to be elected by equal universal suffrage, in direct and secret ballot, or by referendum. The National Assembly would elect from its members a Permanent Commission, which would sit between sessions of the National Assembly. The country was to be administered at local levels through territorial 'collectivities' consisting of communes, arrondissements and administrative regions

Executive power was to reside in the president of the republic, assisted by a cabinet of ministers appointed by him and responsible to him, the president in his turn being responsible to the National Assembly. The president was head of state and supreme commander of the armed forces. He was to be elected, by universal suffrage, for a term of seven years, and could be re-elected for a second term. Any eligible citizen over the age of thirty-five could stand for election.

Title ten of the constitution, headed: 'On the rights and

fundamental duties of citizens,' contained some unusual clauses. It was stated that all citizens should enjoy 'freedom of speech, of press, of assembly, of association, of procession and of public demonstrations under the conditions set by law'. All should enjoy 'the same and equal right to work, rest, social assistance and education. The exercise of trade unionism and the right to strike are recognized for the worker.' Another interesting section of Title Ten was Article 46 which declared that Guinea 'grants the right of sanctuary to foreign citizens pursued because of their struggle for the defence of a just cause, or for their scientific or cultural activities'. Like Ghana, the republic of Guinea soon became a haven for political refugees from other countries, as well as a training base area for African freedom fighters.

As far as international relations were concerned, the preamble of the constitution stated that Guinea adhered to the charter of the United Nations and to the Universal Declaration of Human Rights. It expressed the desire to form 'bonds of friendship with all peoples based on the principles of equality, reciprocal interests and mutual respect of national sovereignty and territorial integrity'. It upheld 'unreservedly all policies tending towards the creation of a United States of Africa and the safeguarding and consolidation of world peace'.

Title Eight of the constitution headed: 'On Inter-African Relations', was however, more significant for panafricanism: 'The Republic may conclude, with any African state, agreements of association or community, comprising partial or complete surrender of sovereignty with a view to achieving African unity.' It was the first time that any African state had written into its constitution such a provision for the surrender of sovereignty. Ghana's republican constitution of March 1960 also contained a similar provision, Article Two stating: 'In the confident expectation of an early surrender of sovereignty to a union of African states and territories the people now confer on parliament the power to provide for the surrender of the whole or any part of the sovereignty of Ghana.'

In fact, Ghana and Guinea made almost identical

declarations about African unification in their republican constitutions. The views of Nkrumah and Sékou Touré on African liberation and unification were virtually the same. They were convinced of the need for political unity before there could be any effective solutions to Africa's fundamental economic problems. Balkanization perpetuated the vicious circle of under-development. The immense human and economic resources of Africa needed to be developed through panafrican planning which could only be effective through unified political machinery. 'The salvation for Africa lies in unity,' said Nkrumah, 'for in unity lies strength, and as I see it African states must unite or sell themselves out to imperialist and neocolonialist exploiters for a mess of pottage, or disintegrate individually.'[5] Most of the small, newly-independent states, with their artificially-created colonial frontiers, had neither the population nor the resources to make them economically viable without massive injections of outside 'aid' which brought with it a new form of exploitation and resulted in the sham independence and puppet governments of neocolonialism. To form regional, economic groupings is not proving to be a satisfactory alternative, since such organizations are just as susceptible to penetration and manipulation by neocolonialists operating through multi-national companies.

But while Nkrumah was distrustful of regional economic organizations because he also considered they obstructed progress towards socialism and continental unification, Sékou Touré had on several occasions been prepared to cooperate in them. The organizations which come immediately to mind in this connection are the Organization of the Senegal River States (O E R S), formed in 1968 between Mali, Guinea, Senegal and Mauritania to promote joint economic, social and cultural development; and the Economic Community of West African States (E C O W A S) formed in 1975 by Benin, Gambia, Guinea, Guinea-Bissau, Ivory Coast, Mali, Mauritania, Niger, Nigeria, Togo, Sierra Leone, Upper Volta, Liberia and Ghana. In the case of O E R S, trouble soon arose between Guinea and the other member states as a result of the Guinean government's conviction that Guinean dissidents were being allowed to carry on their subversive activities in these countries. Guinea withdrew from O E R S in 1971. Lacking common social and economic objectives, and without political machinery to direct and carry out joint economic planning, the organization has achieved very limited results. As regards E C O W A S, it is perhaps too early to assess its significance. Although the Organization was approved by all signatory countries soon after its formation in Lagos on 28 May 1975, it was not until 1977 that the E C O W A S Secretariat and the most important institution of the Community, the Fund for Cooperation, Compensation and Development, were put into operation. Neither Senegal nor Guinea bothered to attend the meeting in Abidjan between 31 May and 14 June 1976 when draft proposals for the Secretariat were being discussed. Guinea was concerned about the reported presence of Israeli and French soldiers in Ivory Coast said to be training Guinean exiles for an invasion of Guinea to overthrow the P D G government. There were disputes between Togo and Benin resulting in the closing of their common border, and quarrels between Togo and Ghana over territory incorporated into Ghana as a result of a plebiscite after Ghana's independence.

It was not a propitious start to the E C O W A S, and it remains to be seen whether the Community functions effectively and for how long. The eminent Egyptian economist Samir Amin, who became director of the African Institute for Economic Development and Planning (I D E P) in 1970, is very critical of the E C O W A S type of economic integration among developing countries. He maintained in 1977 that as long as overall strategy of these countries is outward oriented, the result of their integration is to aggravate unequal development within the region. A sign of this is the migration of people from the poorer hinterland areas of West Africa to the more favoured coastal regions. An economic union based on market rules such as localization of industries within a wider geographical area, and the goal of the highest rate of profit will only worsen the situation, and in Samir Amin's view, further stimulate migration. There has yet to be a long-term successful regional economic organization in Africa. Even the East African Community (E A C) of Kenya, Uganda and Tanzania, set up with so much optimism and promise has finally distintegrated, and for the same basic reasons as the other purely economic groupings, the unsound economic theories on which they were based, the political incompatibility of the governments of the member states, their differing economic and social objectives, and their resulting deep distrust of one another.

By the end of 1958, France had still not given de jure recognition to Guinea. However, Britain, the U S A, Italy, West Germany and most of the other western powers had recognized the new state. Sékou Touré sent a personal representative, Nabi Youla, to Paris to try to persuade de Gaulle to change hi attitude; and he returned to Conakry fairly confident that French official recognition would soon be given. The R D A leadership too, seemed to be modifying its initially hostile view of Guinea. But in the meantime, many countries of the eastern bloc had made agreements with Guinea, and the Ghana–Guinea Union had been signed, thus ending Guinea's political isolation in West Africa.

It was not until January 1959 that relations between Guinea and France improved sufficiently for ambassadors to be exchanged, and for three agreements to be signed. It was agreed that Guinea should remain in the franc zone, and that reciprocal trade preferences should be maintained. There were to be periodic reviews of trade between France and Guinea, when matters such as quotas for imports from third countries could be discussed. French was to continue to be the official language of Guinea, and France undertook to supply teachers. As regards higher education, France agreed to provide facilities for Guinean students to study at French universities. On the technical side, it was agreed that Guinea was to be made eligible for assistance, and that Guinea would seek French technical and administrative personnel before recruiting from elsewhere.

Signature of the agreements was interpreted as French recognition of Guinea. De Gaulle had just become president, and Sékou Touré sent a cable of congratulations: 'We hope that your term of office will bring not only greatness to France, but a tightening of the bonds of cooperation and friendship between our two countries.' The General replied: 'Greatly touched by your message. Like you I express my satisfaction at the protocols regulating our agreements. I send you my best wishes for the Guinean Republic, which is recognized by the French Republic, and I hope the bonds of cooperation between Guinea and France will grow tighter.' If the hope expressed by de Gaulle was sincere, it certainly was not realized in the months that followed. As Guinea's relations with countries of the eastern bloc strengthened; and as Sékou Touré became increasingly convinced that the French secret service was involved in plots against the P D G government, relations between France and Guinea deteriorated sharply. In 1960, France excluded Guinea from the franc zone, and trade between the two countries was almost completely ended.

It was ironic that within three months of Guinea's independence, eleven of the twelve territories of 'French' Africa had indicated their intention to become autonomous republics, and federal members of the Community. Sékou Touré had asked for just such a relationship, but without success. It was only after Guinea had shown that the country could progress as an independent state without France, and after other overseas territories had become autonomous republics that de Gaulle apparently accepted the final demise of the federal community planned in 1958. In a television broadcast on 10 November 1960, he declared: 'In this Community, all the states that compose it are in it because they have chosen it, and all can leave at any moment they choose. It is effective independence and guaranteed cooperation.' The French Assembly had, on 10 May 1960, amended the constitution to allow for the changed character of the Community: 'A member state may by way of agreements, become independent without thereby ceasing to belong to the Community.'

Two new groupings had been formed in West Africa. They were the Mali federation[6] of Soudan and Senegal, and the Entente Council[7] formed by Boigny consisting of Ivory

Coast, Upper Volta and Dahomey. On 5 April 1959 the Great Council of A O F had met for the last time. It handed over its buildings to the federal assembly of Mali, and Senghor was elected president.

The African states ceased to be subject to the Ministry of Overseas France. Yet in spite of all the talk about a French 'federal' community, there was little to make it a reality, there being no federal parliament or federal executive responsible to it. The Executive Council met only seven times between February 1959 and March 1960. The day-to-day work of the Community was carried out by the French Council of Ministers, though matters which were the responsibility of the Community as a whole came under the authority of its president, General de Gaulle, and prime minister Michel Debré. Among the latter's colleagues, until 1960, was Jacques Soustelle, very much mistrusted by Africans as a diehard leader of the Algérie français lobby; and Robert Lecourt (M R P), designated minister of state responsible for economic, financial and cultural relations between France and other member states. Lecourt was therefore in charge of F I D E S, which renamed 'F A C' (Fonds d'Aide et de Co-opération). The Secretariat of the Community was headed successively by two close personal friends of de Gaulle: Raymond Janot, and from February 1960 the notorious Jacques Foccart, considered by Guinea to be behind much of the plotting to overthrow the P D G government.

It was these men who were largely responsible for running Community affairs, though in 1959 de Gaulle did appoint four ministres-counseillers, one for each of the Community's main sectors: Madagascar, A E F, Mali and the Conseil de l'Entente. They were Tsiranana, Lisette, Senghor and Boigny, their role being purely advisory. Likewise, the senate of the Community was, in practice, ineffective, though it was composed of delegates from the legislative assemblies of the member states. The senate met only twice, in July 1959 and June 1960.

At first, de Gaulle refused to recognize the Mali Federation. The result was the demand by Malian leaders for independence and the retention of only confederal links with

France. The suggestion infuriated Boigny, who in September 1959 held an R D A Congress in Abidjan at which he again declared in favour of a federal Community: 'We wish to create a state like the U S S R or the United States ... a multi-national or intercontinental ensemble.' Without the opposition of Sékou Touré, Modibo Keita and d'Arboussier, all of which had left the R D A, Boigny reigned supreme. But even he, as well as de Gaulle, was compelled as time went on to accept the fact that the 'wind of change' in Africa, which British prime minister, Harold Macmillan, was soon to describe in his famous speech of 4 February 1960, made the acceptance of a confederal community inevitable. Addressing the U N General Assembly in November 1959, Boigny said: 'It may be that one day the thirteen Republics which form the Franco-African Community will come to the U N as independent nations; that would in no way weaken the bonds which unite them with the French Republic.' The following month, de Gaulle recognized the Mali Federation: 'Je salue ceux du Mali,' and the executive Council agreed that Mali could become independent without being compelled to leave the Community.

Mali became an independent state within the Community on 20 June 1960, and Madagascar six days later. By then, Boigny had announced that the Entente states would also demand independence. Dahomey became independent on 1 August 1960, Niger on the 3rd, Upper Volta on the 6th and Ivory Coast on the 7th. None of them re-entered the Community, but each signed bilateral cooperation agreements with France. They remained in the franc zone and became associate members of the European Economic Community (E E C). These developments meant the end of the original Franco-African Community, specially since the leaders of the four A E F republics had in their turn also notified de Gaulle that they would ask for independence within the Community. There was no longer any recognizable difference between those African states which were members of it, and those which had not re-entered but had signed bilateral agreements.

On 20 August 1960, Senegal suddenly seceded from the

Mali Federation. Many had predicted that the federation would not last, because there were basic differences between the two states. The disciplined, radical policies of Modibo Keita's government were mistrusted by the more easy-going Senegalese. In addition, the Senegalese feared that the Soudanese aspired to absorb Senegal since they appeared to be increasing their influence in Senegal's domestic affairs. The immediate cause of the break-up, however, was over the question of the election of a president for the federal republic. The Senegalese insisted on Senghor, while the Soudanese considered him unsuitable. It was the final straw. Senegal and Soudan went their separate ways and Soudan became the Republic of Mali. Agreements with France were broken off and in December 1960 Mali joined the Ghana-Guinea Union.

In September 1960, France sponsored the admission to the UN of twelve independent African states.[8] In doing so, the French government had accepted the failure of the attempt to preserve the French empire through a Franco-African Community. Henceforward, France would adopt a new strategy to maintain the economic and strategic benefits of empire without exercising direct political control. This would involve the continuance of close economic ties with the former territories of the French Community; and the support, by military means if necessary, of francophone governments. The new republics had chosen 'association' rather than 'community' with France. De Gaulle considered the transformation acceptable as it 'in no way undermined our interests, merely altering the form without affecting the basis of Franco-African solidarity'.[9]

All the French-speaking states of West Africa, apart from Guinea and Mali, at that time supported the view of Senghor and Boigny, that close links should be maintained with France, and that economic cooperation between African states must precede any plans for political unity. It was all the more remarkable, therefore, that Ghana and Guinea were able, as early as November 1958 to declare the Ghana-Guinea Union which was to be a pilot scheme for a wider union of African states. The Ghana-Guinea Union provided for resident ministers to be exchanged who were to be members of both the governments of Ghana and Guinea. It was an imaginative, bold initiative, cutting across differences of language, institutions, culture and colonial background.

When in November 1958, Sékou Touré and Nkrumah signed the Ghana–Guinea Union declaration at the end of Sékou Touré's five-day visit to Accra, the initial reaction in London and Paris was one of mutual recrimination. British and Commonwealth governments feared that Nkrumah might intend to bring Guinea into the Commonwealth. The French press, on the other hand, suspected that the Union would not have been agreed without the secret, prior approval of Britain which was also suspected of having agreed to Ghana making the £10 million loan[10] to Guinea to enable her to survive the sudden withdrawal of French economic support at independence. The £10 million represented just under 4 per cent of the national income of Ghana, and was made at a time when Ghana was launching its own development plans. It was, therefore, a particularly generous action which could only be understood within the context of genuine and practical panafricanism. But not all Ghanaians agreed with it. Kofi Busia, leader of the opposition United Party, opposed it on the grounds that the money was needed for development projects in the northern territories of Ghana. He also opposed the Ghana–Guinea Union, declaring that if his party came to power it would 'disregard' it. His declaration coming as it did some two weeks before the opening of the historic All-African Peoples' Conference in Accra on 5 December 1958, was badly timed and ran quite contrary to the spirit of panafricanism pervading Accra.

Shortly after the formation of the Ghana–Guinea Union, Ghana sent a team of economic and financial experts to Guinea to study the country's economic problems, and to discuss plans for economic cooperation. There were rumours that ways were being sought for Guinea to enter the sterling zone, not simply because of the alliance with Ghana, but in view of France's failure to settle financial arrangements with Guinea. But these rumours ceased abruptly when a team of financial experts was hurriedly sent to Conakry by the French government to discuss conditions for Guinea's continuance in the franc zone, and to try to resolve other outstanding economic issues between the two countries.

In a joint communique issued at the end of the Ghanaian economic mission's visit to Conakry, Ghana and Guinea agreed to appoint a joint commission to study economic and financial problems; measures to coordinate foreign policies and establish and improve communications between them by radio, air and sea; and a constitutional committee to work out a United States of West Africa. The French financial mission was still in Guinea when the Ghanaian team left, and Guinea had undertaken to remain for the time being in the franc zone.

Gradually, Guinea emerged as a leading, progressive and panafrican state as a result of the reputation and performance of the P D G as a genuinely people's party. For the P D G definition of democracy goes farther than the general conception in that it involves not merely government by consent, but the according of the initiative to the people. 'There are two ways of governing a country,' declared Sékou Touré. 'In the first way, the state may substitute itself for all initiative, all men, all conscience. At that moment, it deprives the people of their liberty of initiative, places them under conditions, and in consequence passes itself off as omniscient by trying to solve general problems, and problems of details simultaneously. Such a state can only be anti-democratic and oppressive. We have adopted the second way and chosen to be a democratic state.'[11] The faith of the leaders of the P D G in the people, and the faith of the people in themselves would', an observer said, 'save Guinea from any possible error'.[12] Sékou Touré endorsed this view: 'The determining basis of the great victories of the P D G,' he said, 'is the absolute confidence in the infinite capacity of the people.'

Nevertheless, a gigantic task of total mobilization of people and resources had to be embarked upon. Guinea was at independence, according to Sékou Touré, a 'juridically constituted state without historical identity'.[13] The country had the artificial frontiers of colonialism, and comprised peoples of different ethnic, religious and linguistic groupings. It was necessary to construct a unified nation and to develop the economy to raise the standard of living of every sector of the population. Referring to the P D G policy of ethnic integration, Sékou Touré said that there would be 'no more in the Republic of Guinea the Malinké race, the Soussou race, the Foulah race, the Guerzé race, the Landouma or Kissi race ... Every youth of Guinea, every adult of Guinea, asked about his race will reply that he is "African".'[14] The former colony had to be transformed into a nation.

Colonial structures were toppled at all levels, and new structures created by the people of Guinea. The first six months after independence were devoted to national conferences. Everything had to be questioned and adapted or changed to meet the new situation. The civil code, for example, was drafted and submitted to every village. There were lawyers who scorned the idea of consulting the peasantry. However, the draft code was translated into the various national languages and discussed throughout the towns and villages of Guinea. When at length the civil code was finally agreed it could be said to reflect the will of the people. Educational and commercial reforms were similarly submitted to all sectors of the population. The process of what Sékou Touré has described as 'self-realization, self-administration and self-management' is necessarily lengthy and continuing. It must be methodically organized, and develop in accordance with principles and objectives decided by the people.

The P D G, until independence a territorial wing of the R D A, had to shed the R D A connection and to adapt to become the independent party of government. Changes in organization and policy would be required. The preamble to the statutes of the P D G[15] declares that the party is:

> Resolved to remain a popular party, the effective agent of political, economic and social promotion based on the action of the masses, the inexhaustible source of creative energies.

On the basis of the mass line, the PDG is resolved, thanks to the cultural and socialist revolution, to carry out a radical transformation of mentalities and to root out from the society all irrational practices, all alienating tendencies, and the slightest inclination towards the exploitation of man by man.

The PDG recognizes class struggle as the only dynamic and historically just step towards the conquest of political, economic, social and cultural power by the entire people.

The 'guiding principle' of the PDG was to be democratic centralism, which means according to the PDG:

a) Election of all the directing bodies of the party from the base to the summit

b) Periodic accounts of the bodies of the party for their respective purposes and before the immediately superior directing bodies

c) Rigorous discipline in the party and submission of the minority to the majority.

To ensure mass participation in political processes there is a clearly defined line of communication from village and regional levels to the summit. Party and state, party and people are fused so that the party becomes the party-state. At the summit of party structure are four bodies, the national congress responsible for the broad outlines of party policy, and summoned at least once every five years; the national council of the revolution (CNR), which acts as the supreme party institution between sessions of the congress, and is summoned about twice a year; the central committee consisting of twenty-five members elected by the congress for a five-year term, and which meets monthly; and the national political bureau (BPN), meeting fortnightly, the executive body of the central committee, consisting of seven members including the secretary-general of the PDG who proposes the names of the six other members. The secretary-general is elected for a five-year term by the congress.

At the base of party organization are the local revolutionary authorities, the *'pouvoirs révolutionnaires locaux'*

(P R Ls). Each village, and every *'quartier'* in towns, constitutes a P R L making some 8,000 in all throughout Guinea. Every P R L has a thirteen member executive elected every two years. The P R Ls, meeting weekly, are grouped within 210 sections constituting the next level of party structure. Again, each section has a thirteen member executive, called a steering committee, which is elected every two years by executive members of its constituent P R L. Then come the thirty federations, each with a thirteen member executive known as a federal bureau, elected every three years by members of the constituent steering committees.

The decision to create P R Ls was taken at a meeting of the P D G central committee in Kankan between 30 October and 3 November 1967. The meeting followed the Eighth Congress of the P D G when the 'radicalization' of the revolution and the formal adoption of 'socialism' was agreed. Guinea had become a party-state, by P D G definition a country in which the state, the technical instrument of the people is merged with the party, a political instrument of the people. Public services, justice, education, health, communications, land distribution and utilization, trade and so on, which reflect the collective interest of villagers are in the hands of the people themselves. At regional level, only the governor is, for the time being nominated. All other cadres are elected. At national level, all members of the central committee are elected by congress though the head of state may make use of 'efficient, non-elected cadres' in technical posts. Thus it is the people who decide, implement and control. It is the people who elect administrators at all levels of the party and the state apparatus. The reality of power being theirs, anyone who attempts to subvert the revolutionary ethic may be dismissed at any time by popular will.

The pyramidal structure, therefore, is designed to provide for the sovereignty of the people and their full participation in government at every level, and in all its aspects. It is not yet perfected. It remains to abolish the bureaucracy, the bourgeoisie as a class, and other 'forces of resistance' to the popular will. For the Guinean revolution proceeds inexorably, unfolding and developing as the people decide, and at the pace determined by them. Eventually the state will wither away, and the conquest of power by the people will be complete. According to the P D G, 'the time of triumphant socialism will come, when there will be no more reality based on human exploitation. Everybody will have identified himself with it, interpreting its laws and principles, defending its objective. This phase of homogeneity of the whole people corresponds to the transformation and merger of all the people in their infinite improvement, into a single class, the people's class, with the people then assuming all the attributes of the state.'[16]

In the smallest villages, African affairs, problems of international relations, as well as day-to-day Guinean matters are discussed. Opinions and suggestions made at P R L level are considered at section and federation level, passing through to central organs of the party. A law or a major policy decision is only promulgated after it has been discussed, understood and accepted at the level of the smallest organs of the party. For in the words of Sékou Touré: 'The party constitutes the thought of the people of Guinea in its highest level and in its most complete form. The thought of the party indicates the orientation of our actions; the thought of the party specifies the principles which direct our behaviour, our collective and individual attitude.'[17] The P D G is the definer of the general interest, the custodian of the popular will, expressing the collective thought of the Guinean people.

From federalism, the P D G proceeded along the path of radicalism and panafricanism, though the implementation of long-term economic and political objectives would depend to some extent upon the solution of short-term difficulties. If Guinea could survive the first year or so, then the chances were that the confidence of the people in themselves would prove well-justified. 'It may be thought that, hypnotized by the magic of words we have chosen freedom for the sake of independence,' said Sékou Touré, 'whereas we have chosen freedom for the sake of our dignity, and independence in order that African unity can be achieved. Transcending the conditions created by colonialism, we have posed not the problem of Guinea, still less the problem of a party or a man. But we have posed with clarity the true problem, the sole problem, of Africa.'[18]

The P D G resigned from the R D A in October 1958. The move was hastened by the R D A's decision to press for Guinea's exclusion from the party at the November meeting of its coordination committee. The R D A executive considered that the R D A had acted in the best interests of Africans by recommending a 'Yes' vote in the referendum; and that the P D G had 'gravely offended' by choosing in effect 'independence through secession'. Another factor was a declaration of Boigny, president of the R D A, that he regarded the Franco-African Community as an end in itself, and not merely a stepping stone to the full sovereignty and independence of the overseas territories. This declaration had made any continuation of links between the P D G and R D A impossible. Boigny's declaration also angered the P R A, which decided to go ahead on its own to plan for the independence of the territories and for federations of A O F and A E F.

Although Guinea had rejected de Gaulle's constitution, it had not ruled out the idea of some kind of association with France. Within the P D G there was, and remained, a pro-French lobby. To this small but influential group it has always made sense not to shut the door on France completely. Trading connections, social and cultural traditions, administrative structures, all had been fashioned to a greater or lesser degree by the French. Total isolation from France would therefore mean a fundamental break with the historical past, which would at least in the short-term cause immense difficulties. In addition, it would make it impossible for Guinea to continue in association with her near neighbours Ivory Coast, Senegal, Mauritania, Niger, Upper Volta and Soudan, all of which remained within the French community. For them, the problem posed by independent Guinea was how to establish satisfactory relations with France as an equal, sovereign state. 'Sékou Touré himself said at the time of the referendum that Guinea was voting 'No' to the constitution but 'Yes' to France. Four days before the referendum took place, Sékou Touré had approached Governor Mauberna with an application for association with the Community under Article 88 of the constitution. According to Sékou Touré: 'From the moment of our independence, without acrimony, without preconceived ideas, we have held out our hands to France. What we wanted, and what we still want, is that new relationships may be established between the French nation and the young Guinea nation to the great advantage of both peoples.'[19]

In spite, therefore, of Sékou Touré's personal dislike of de Gaulle, a feeling of mistrust which was mutual, the Guinea government requested a treaty of association with France at the same time as it asked the French government for a formal transfer of sovereignty. De Gaulle replied that France could take no decision until it was assured that Guinea was able to exercise 'the charges and obligations of sovereignty and independence'. The general wanted to know precisely what kind of association Guinea had in mind. It would be necessary, he said, to consult first with the organs of the future federal community. De Gaulle was supported in this by Boigny, who took the view that any association between independent Guinea and the Community was a matter which the overseas territories should decide. On the other hand, Senghor and Apithy were in favour of accepting Guinea's request for 'association'. But it was Boigny who had the greater influence with de Gaulle.

While pressing the French government for recognition and for 'association', Sékou Touré asked France to sponsor Guinea's application to become a member of the United Nations. He received no reply, and Guinea's membership was therefore proposed by Japan and Iraq, and seconded by Ghana and Haiti. On 9 December 1958, the Security Council voted to admit Guinea. Four days later, on 12 December, the General Assembly followed suit. In each case the decision was unanimous, though France abstained from voting in the Security Council and in the General Assembly.

Within weeks of Guinea's independence it had become clear that there were radical differences between the policies and objectives of the countries of the French Community and Guinea, which would make an association acceptable to both extremely unlikely. At the core of the problems between France and Guinea were the practical questions of the payment of pensions for Guinean ex-servicemen by France, and Guinean compensation for nationalized enterprises. French public investment in Guinea ceased, and the French government tried to stop private firms from investing there.

As the months went by and the P D G's political and economic programmes began to be implemented, many Guineans went into voluntary exile either in France, or in one or other of the neighbouring states. These, along with reactionaries who chose to remain in Guinea, and Guinean soldiers who decided to continue in the French forces after independence, were to form the main body of those who have supported subversion against the P D G government ever since independence. In general, they were from the professional and business *élite* who stood to lose the most as a result of P D G policies, and the break with France. While the majority were in favour of self-government they did not wish to see a radical transformation of society.

Practically every state emerging from conditions of colonialism has had to face a similar problem caused by the indigenous, privileged sector opposing the measures necessary to raise the standard of living of the people as a whole. In the ex-British colonies, this privileged sector, usually prominent in the broad front of the national liberation movement, either succeeded at independence in going on to form the party of government, or split away to form an opposition determined to prevent the destruction of capitalist social and economic structures. It was largely the problems raised by the presence of backward-looking members of national liberation movements which caused consideration to be given to the formation of vanguard parties in some progressive states after independence. For example, the 'vanguard activists' in Ghana; and in Mozambique, the 'Marxist Leninist vanguard party' of the workers and peasants created through a decision reached by the Third Congress of Frelimo in February 1977. The broad front of the pre-independence period, necessary in order to end colonial rule, could not adapt to provide the radical government needed if the fruits of independence were to be enjoyed by all the people. Arguments for and against the mass party or the vanguard party continue to occupy political theorists, the conclusions reached depending much on the view taken of the class struggle. Meantime, most of the remaining civilian governments of Africa have found it necessary to become one-party states.

In Guinea, the P D G began, and continued after independence as a mass party, though as time went on the need arose to re-examine conditions of membership as part of the P D G's crack down on bourgeois elements. From being a mass party which included practically the entire population, membership of the P D G became in 1964 restricted to 'activists who have proved themselves'. Qualities required for membership included a grasp of socialist ideology, devotion to the socialist cause, ability to organize, honesty, self-sacrifice and a simple life-style. Care was given to the class composition of the party, only the most revolutionary elements, workers, peasants, revolutionary intelligentsia and 'outsiders' who were ideologically sound being included.

Even in those states such as Mozambique and Angola, where the national liberation movements took the form of a guerrilla struggle, and where the party of the freedom fighters became the party of government at independence, problems caused by indigenous privileged groups have continued to hamper the implementation of progressive policies. Nkrumah described these people as a small, selfish, money-minded, reactionary minority among vast masses of exploited and oppressed people'.[20] They were the ready made agents of neocolonialists, and formed the makings of a fifth column embedded within the newly-independent state.

Sékou Touré in analysing the class structure of Guinean society speaks of the 'people's class' and the 'anti-people class'. The former, which represents some 90 per cent of the people, includes various strata, and within each there are social categories. It is informed, mobilized and educated by the P D G, the party of the revolution, and does not live on human exploitation but on the 'exploitation of nature'. The people's class are peasants, workers, traders, fishermen, farmers, and all who strive to fulfil the aspirations of the people. Among this class social categories are distinguished from one another by the quality or importance of the means of production at their disposal. Internal contradictions emerge within these strata as economically dominant categories appear, but these will remain minor if the necessary measures leading to social progress are taken and implemented by the revolutionary vanguard party, so that eventually a classless society is constructed.

The anti-people class include industrialists, merchants, 'ill-reputed functionaries,' corrupt officers, deposed feudal elements, and all those unwilling to adapt to the new conditions replacing feudal-colonial structures. These people look backwards towards feudalism and 'have no other dream than that of substituting themselves for the European colonialists in order to be able to exploit the Guinean people'.[21]

The class struggle content of PDG ideology was not emphasized during the period of the national liberation struggle since it was fused with the anti-imperialist struggle. But the two cannot be separated, even after independence is achieved. For the anti-imperialist struggle 'is the climax of the antagonistic contradiction opposing us to neo-colonialism, colonialism, capitalism and feudalism ... Thus class struggle must be carried in all directions, against all basic oppositions and contradictions, and at the same time against the causes of internal contradictions ... The revolutionaries of Africa know that imperialism is the highest stage of capitalism, and that the anti-imperialist struggle is the climax of class struggle.'[22]

The PDG then, is aware that a great number of contradictions emerge within any party, and will continue to emerge. For where there is life there are contradictions. But the PDG, through organization and political education aims to defeat the forces of counter-revolution. Therefore, while recognizing class distinctions and contradictions it prepares the political ground for their liquidation.

7

DEVELOPMENT

WHILE the P D G considers some African governments have become 'true artisans' in the building of the new Africa, others have maintained the basic economic and social structures of colonialism. In Guinea, the P D G, after consolidating the period of 'national democracy', has proceeded towards 'popular democracy' through the radicalization of the party. Initially, after independence, Guineans spoke of a 'non-capitalist' path of development, and critics of the P D G questioned the meaning of the term, asking: 'Why not socialist development?' The P D G maintained that it was more courageous to use the term 'non-capitalist' than to lecture on 'socialist development'. It was a time when there was much talk of 'African socialism', which according to Senghor appeared to be a 'socialism' compatible with capitalism. Sékou Touré and the P D G did not wish to be associated in any way with such a bogus concept. They preferred, therefore, for the time being to refer to the Guinean path of development as being 'non-capitalist', implying the adoption of genuinely socialist policies. As Sékou Touré declared in a speech to the Sixth Congress of the P D G in 1962: 'Our way is a non-capitalist way. It will remain so because this way is the only one which safeguards the interests of the community while freeing individuals from the injustice which characterizes all relations of exploitation of man by man.' Subsequently, as the myth of 'African socialism' was exposed, and the P D G progressed towards a radicalization of the party, the terminology of the Guinean revolution adjusted accordingly to include the term 'socialism' to describe the general objective of the party.

There has been much spoken and written by Sékou Touré

and members of the P D G central committee and others on the question of 'development'. It is a recurring theme in most of the volumes of the works of the P D G, while some of the volumes are exclusively devoted to it. Volume V published in 1960, and called 'Economic Development' deals entirely with economic problems and policies. So also does Volume XIV on the Seven Year Development Plan (1964–71). In Volume X, called 'Africa in Motion', and published in 1967, over a hundred pages are devoted to the same subject. Volume XVI, entitled 'Popular Power' contains many chapters on the economy. Volume XX treats economic matters in more detail; and Volume XXI, published in 1977 summarizes the economic policies of the P D G in a lengthy section called simply 'Development'. In this book it is made clear that Sékou Touré and the P D G regard economics as an aspect of politics, and therefore subject to party supremacy. 'We shall have the economy of our politics and not the politics of our economy.'[1]

The P D G distinguishes between economic growth and development. 'There is development when economic growth is homogeneous, and effectively ensures quantitative and qualitative progress in all fields of the people's life; in the material, medical, educational, cultural fields, including science and technology ... But when the change is partial, covering only one sector of the economy, or even several limited sectors, such an economic growth must not be confused with true development ... Economic development always goes with economic growth, while the reverse is not always true. Development always implies growth. When the latter is general, even and harmonious, it becomes synonymous with development.'[2]

To achieve the objectives of the P D G, development must be both planned and implemented by the people themselves, and at a pace which they determine. The P D G rejects the capitalist approach which separates areas of development between different sectors of the population. This brings about an internal imbalance and sacrifices the welfare of the people as a whole.

Western economists are prone to compare unfavourably

the economy of Guinea with that of other countries in West Africa, notably Ivory Coast. Such comparisons are not accepted by the P D G since they refer only to economic growth and not overall development. Guineans measure progress not in capitalist terms of profit and the enrichment of minority sectors of the population, but in socialist terms of the level of political, economic, social and cultural well-being of the people as a whole. A neocolony can, according to capitalist thinking, be showing economic growth, while a state determined to be genuinely independent, and interested only in balanced development to raise the standard of living of the population as a whole, can in some cases be shown to have achieved a comparatively slow rate of economic growth. The P D G states that independent, economic development implies that the objectives of development, and the organization and control of labour, must be determined and implemented by the people themselves, and the fruits of labour be distributed according to social justice. Development, therefore, is not only harmonious and balanced, but it is absolutely independent, based solely on the will of the people, and for their exclusive benefit. Self-reliance is key. 'We can never build a man's happiness without his own participation.'[3] Self-reliance must operate at all levels, from the village to national level. This is not to exclude foreign help, but only aid which helps Guinea to do without aid is acceptable. Aid which becomes more and more necessary transforms the recipient from a friend into an employee, to a slave, and finally into an alien in his own land. For where economic development is not independent it is 'alienated'.

According to the P D G, Ivory Coast is a country in which economic development is alienated, and where 'there is no development in the true sense of the word',[4] in spite of their impressive sounding trade figures. To whom does the wealth belong? Up to 40 per cent of investment in industry in Ivory Coast is controlled by French groups, and at least 50 per cent of investment in trade is French. At the end of a visit to Ivory Coast by the French President Giscard d'Estaing in January 1978, it was announced that French companies had signed contracts with Ivory Coast worth 2·8 billion francs (£300 million) since the beginning of January 1976. There were, it was stated, about 45,000 French nationals in Ivory Coast, over four times as many as at independence.

Far from considering Ivory Coast as 'rich', Guineans regard the country as 'backward'. The wealth is largely owned by foreigners and the indigenous bourgeoisie, while in Guinea, land and the means of production belong to the people. In Ivory Coast, government ministers live like kings. A Guinean minister earns three times less than a principal secretary in Ivory Coast, and five times less than his Ivorian counterpart. In fact, every minister in Ivory Coast earns three times more than the President of Guinea. Sékou Touré and the P D G are proud of their low salaries and small houses. Any Guinean minister who made a fortune would be instantly 'crushed by the people of Guinea whom he had robbed'.

In all things, the happiness and well-being of the people must come first. The process of development followed by societies usually called 'developed', which have achieved great technological progress has not created the conditions which permit free and full human development. Such societies are obsessed by economic matters, which they separate from political and social considerations. They may be strong and well developed materially and technologically, but they can be less developed than societies in which the human element is uppermost. The large part of the world labelled 'underdeveloped' by those who measure development in terms of material profit and the organizations founded on it, has no need, for example, of old peoples' homes and orphanages and other characteristic institutions of socially backward societies. For the P D G yardstick for measuring development is how far the human potential and human needs have been fulfilled. This cannot be shown in terms of statistics or on charts showing economic performance. It can only be experienced or observed in the degree to which the people's interests are being served.

In Guinea, as in other ex-colonial territories, political development preceded economic and social development, the ending of colonial rule being the prerequisite for any

The Almamy Samory Touré

A PDG meeting

Women members of the PDG in front of the President's residence in Conakry

Bauxite mining

Young technician at the Friguia bauxite mining complex

meaningful progress. 'The result of this,' according to Sékou Touré, 'is that all our human activities have constant political control and guidance ... The greatest strength of the Guinean revolution is in fact its political thought, which makes use of all social phenomena and activities of national life to serve the exclusive interest of the people.'[5] It is not a narrowly nationalist view of development. For the PDG considers it no longer acceptable for any people or any nation to think exclusively of its own development. 'We should, and such is our ambition, participate in the solution of the problems which beset all humanity. We have repeatedly said that the general conditions of the human race must necessarily have a bearing on the particular conditions of development of our own society, just as what our society does must have a bearing in the development of other societies.'[6]

Guinea allows foreign capitalist investment in the great economic potential of the country, but it is strictly limited and controlled. Guinea has a fertile soil and vast mineral resources. All regions have an abundant water supply. Guinea has been called the 'water tower' of West Africa, and the country has enormous hydro-electric power possibilities. Guinea has probably the best economic potential of the whole of West Africa, and the PDG plans to develop it to the full for the benefit of all the people. Guinea's resources could have been offered to neocolonialists on their terms. But Guineans rejected neocolonialism, or prosperity in slavery, with the famous 'No' vote on 28 September 1958. 'We have foregone irresponsibility and indignity. We are determined to assume full responsibility for own future.'[7] Since the people own the means of production, determine the nature of the relations of production, and decide the distribution of their productivity, they are the exclusive agent and at the same time the sole beneficiary of a development which is democratic, popular and revolutionary. Foreign capital, therefore, enters Guinea under stringent conditions, and in no way is it allowed to hamper socialist objectives. In the words of Sékou Touré: 'We shall work with those who accept our conditions.'

There are in Guinea, three sectors of development, a

national sector, a joint-venture sector in which the Guinean people are associated with foreign partners for the development of a portion of the natural resources, and a small private sector. Indigenous private enterprise is allowed in areas not concerned with nationally-owned resources and public services, though it is not actively encouraged. The purpose is to expand the public sector and to keep the private sector to a minimum.

In Guinea, some 80–85 per cent of the people are engaged in agriculture, animal husbandry and fishing. Rural development, therefore, which mobilizes some four-fifths of the working people, constitutes the basis of the country's economic development programme. Its objective is to provide the food the people need, raw materials and crops for industry, and for export to bring in the funds to finance industrialization and essential imports. An indication of the importance attached to agriculture is shown in the eleven ministries dealing with rural development. In addition, in each region there is a 'regional development conference' and a 'regional council of the revolution' to coordinate and administer the work of village agricultural production brigades and P R Ls. All cadres concerned with the party's agricultural and animal husbandry plans meet regularly to discuss problems, to consider results, and to devise ways to increase production. Difficulties and shortcomings are not minimized, but are openly admitted and discussed. Many different schemes to modernize and collectivize the agricultural sector have been tried out. In the first development plan, the Three Year Plan agreed by the Second National Congress in Kankan in April 1960, twenty state farms were to be established, and modernization centres (C M Rs) and cooperatives (C A Ps) were to be created in rural areas. Targets were set for the main export crops of bananas, coffee, palm oil products and groundnuts. But results were disappointing, production falling well below the targets set. In the Seven Year Plan (1964–71), again targets were set which for various reasons were not attained, and the P D G changed and modified local organizations to improve productivity. The Seven Year Plan, unlike the Three Year Plan which was drawn up by French economists because of the lack of trained economists in Guinea, was the result of proposals put forward by party organizations from P R L to federation level, and government departments. In keeping with the constant aim of the P D G, that Guinea shall become self-sufficient in food, the purpose of the plan as far as the agricultural sector was concerned, was to increase the rate of modernization and therefore productivity. The current Five Year Plan, launched in 1973, emphasizes the same point, that Guinea must produce enough food so that it is no longer necessary to import it. The annual cost of food imports currently represents the purchase value of some 4,000 tractors, spare parts and the fuel and oil needed to operate them. Guinea has the necessary resources to achieve self-sufficiency. It is, therefore, a question of developing them to the full through hard work and scientific, intensive farming techniques. Production brigades, both mechanized (B M Ps) and non-mechanized (B A Ps) have been created throughout rural Guinea. Each B M P aims to farm a minimum of 120 hectares, 90 of rice, 20 of cassava, and 10 of groundnuts. Every P R L becoming an economic unit has a B M P and a B A P. 'The rural production brigade is an economic institution the importance of which reflects the decisive role played within every village community by the P R L, as an expression of the reality of the sovereignty recovered, organized and directly exercised by and for the people in all spheres of their existence.'[8] Before the establishment of collective production brigades, farming was largely on a family scale and at subsistence level. There were as many farms as there were families in a village, each farm being only about two or three hectares in size. Now, not only is land owned collectively, but it is also farmed collectively. Increased productivity through mechanization should eventually enable the brigades to be self-financing. Meantime, the cost of workers' pay, the supply of seeds, fertilizers and other investment needs including farm machinery, is provided by the government as a loan to be repaid after the harvest.

Rice is the staple food of Guinea, and rice production is therefore key in the drive towards self-sufficiency. In a survey of the economy in May 1975, Sékou Touré reported that only 20,000 tons of rice had to be imported that year, while 60,000 tons were imported in 1974. He hoped that it might be possible to stop importing rice entirely within a few years, and so make a very valuable saving in foreign exchange. Other sectors were also expected to show improvement. The production figure for palm products was estimated at 25,000 tons in 1975, whereas it had been only 8,000 tons in 1974; coffee production was expected to exceed 10,000 tons; the production of bananas, pineapples, orange juice and so on, was similarly expected to increase. Agriculture, in general, seemed to be showing considerable improvement, so that the party's target of being able to dispense with the need to import food might be attainable in the not too distant future, 'Violà l'objectif,' declared Sékou Touré. The future, he said, depended on the success of the agricultural production brigades. In five to ten years, they should have worked in such a way that no peasant would consider it preferable to farm on his own rather than as a member of the collective organization of the P R L and the production brigade. In 1975, some 434 mechanized production brigades were created and equipped with seeds, machinery, fertilizers and so on, to enable them to produce the prescribed quantities of crops. The production of rice was increasing to such an extent that the P D G expected Guinea might soon have enough to meet domestic requirements and have some to spare for other African countries. The plan was for every village to have a production brigade. These and the revolutionary education centres (C E Rs), will eventually fuse with the P R Ls to form self-supporting 'socialist communities'.

Just as in the political sphere, it is the policy of the P D G to decentralize, so also in the domain of the economy. There is regional and local budgeting and accountability. If production targets are not met, the reasons are investigated at P R L and regional levels. Production brigades in different areas help one another by exchanging ideas and experience. But Sékou Touré is constantly warning against excessive theorizing. 'Meetings of cadres, still less wise words and demonstrations cannot satisfy the needs of the nation. Production contributing to the rise in the standard of living of the people is what counts. Production is the fundamental and permanent requirement of the revolution.'[19]

Guinea's rural development programme, assisted initially by Chinese experts, and now based on the P R Ls and the production brigades, continues to progress in spite of difficulties most of which are common to other countries of the so called third world. There is shortage of money to buy much-needed farm machinery, fertilizers and other necessities; there are insufficient trained agricultural workers, and traditional methods of farming die hard; crop diseases, periods of drought, the vagaries of world markets, smuggling, inefficiency, and in some cases deliberate acts of economic sabotage through corrupt officials and traders have all contributed at times to slow up the implementation of P D G rural development plans. In addition, Guinea has not been immune from the effects of world recession and inflation. Like other producers of raw materials, subject to world market prices over which they have little or no control, Guinea has had to face constantly rising prices of essential imports. In such circumstances, the most meticulously prepared development plans are liable to be thwarted. The P D G's preparedness to modify and adapt policies as conditions change has stood it in good stead in economic planning. For example, partly as a result of assessing the urgent need to provide more funds for the better equipping of rural production brigades, the Guinea government imposed in 1975 an export tax on minerals and their derivatives. The new tax was expected to bring in some 4,800,000 U S dollars. The Guinea Bauxite Company (C B G) was expected to export a minimum of five million tons of bauxite in 1975, the Bauxite office of Kindia (O B K) some two million tons, and the Fria complex, now F R I G U I A, about 660,000 tons of alumina. Thus the industrial sector, financed largely by foreign companies and governments, helps to fund agricultural development which is mainly dependent on local savings.

At independence, there was very little industrial development apart from the Fria mining complex, financed by a consortium of five companies, the main shareholder being the American firm Olin Matheson Chemical Corporation which had a 48·5 per cent holding. The French company Pechiney held 26·5 per cent of the shares; the British Aluminium Company and the Swiss Aluminium Industrie Aktiengesellschaft 10 per cent each; and the German company Vereinigte Aluminium Werke 5 per cent. Fria's history in fact goes back to 1942 when prospecting for bauxite began in the region of Kindia. At that time, the Canadian Aluminium Company was planning bauxite production on the Los islands, opposite Conakry. In 1956, Fria drew up a detailed plan for alumina production in the Kindia-Konkouré region where bauxite deposits are estimated at some 140 million tons; and the Guinea government signed an agreement with Fria giving tax concessions in the initial period, and guaranteeing certain financial and legal conditions for a period of seventy-five years. The giant alumina factory was to employ over 6,000 people and to convert bauxite into alumina at the eventual rate of one million tons a year. Until February 1973, Fria was a private enterprise. But then the Guinea government entered into partnership when F R I G U I A was formed, taking 49 per cent ownership and 65 per cent of the profits.

New bauxite mines were opened at Boké in 1973 with the formation of the Guinea Bauxite Company, owned 49 per cent by Guinea and 51 per cent by western capitalist interests. Three other bauxite projects, at Dabola, Kindia and Tougué, were under construction, each of them the result of cooperation between the Guinea government and foreign firms and governments. The Dabola project is in association with Yugoslavia, the Kindia project, which began producing in November 1973, and has an annual capacity of three million tons, is in cooperation with the U S S R; and the project at Tougué with Swiss participation. Soon, if production targets are met, Guinea will become the world's largest producer of bauxite. The new port of Kamsar is already the world's most important bauxite-exporting port with an annual capacity of nine million tons, the open cast mine at Sangarady being linked to the port by a new 153 kilometre railway. This mining complex required a 310 million dollar investment which was obtained through the World Bank. Guinea is associated in the project with the principal aluminium producers – Alcan, Alcoa, Harvey, Pechiney, Aluminium-Werke, and Montecatini Edison, Guinea having 65 per cent share of the profits.

In 1977, the Guinea government entered into negotiations with a consortium of Arab countries[10] to finance the large Ayekoyé bauxite deposits estimated at some 500 million tons. The project aims at first producing two million tons of alumina and later 150,000 tons of aluminium. It is hoped that the Konkouré dam will provide the necessary low cost electricity.

In 1958, electricity production in Guinea was estimated at twenty million kilowatts. By 1968, production was up to 202 million kilowatts about three-quarters of which was being used by Guinea's growing industries. Electricity has been supplied virtually to the whole of middle and upper Guinea through the building of dams with foreign assistance, though much of Guinea's hydro-electric potential is still untapped. At independence, a preliminary study of the Konkouré dam project had been made by the French colonial government. But the documents were among those removed when the French withdrew. In 1965, an agreement was signed with the U S S R for reactivating the project. But it was not until 1971 that definite progress was made when an Italian firm agreed to construct the dam. It is estimated that an annual output of 150,000 tons of aluminium can eventually be produced by building an aluminium smelting project using electric power from Konkouré which is expected to provide 6000 million kilowatts.

Apart from bauxite, Guinea has another large mineral resource, namely iron ore. Deposits estimated at 300 million tons, with an iron content of 65–67 per cent are located in the mountains of Nimba-Simendou. These are to be mined by the Société des mines de fer de Guinée (Mifergui). Though iron ore is likely to become an important Guinean export, bauxite is still the chief export. Probably about 90 per cent of Guinea's exports will still be bauxite by 1985, and this raises both problems of over-dependence on world markets and possibly indigenous neocolonialist pressures which may threaten domestic freedoms.

Under the Three Year Development Plan only about 21 per cent of total investments were for the industrial sector; and of this just over 7 per cent had been spent by the end of the Plan period. Among the projects were a cigarettes and matches factory, a sawmill, a canning factory for fruit and meat, a furniture factory, a printing press and a diamond mining enterprise. In the Seven Year Plan, the industrial sector received more attention. Among the projects to be established were factories for processing groundnut oil, coconut oil, palm oil and other by-products, bicycle, motor vehicle and radio assembly plants, a petroleum refinery, a sugar refinery, cement factory, ceramic and paper factories, a glass factory, aluminium smelter, fertilizer factory and a steel mill. All did not materialize. But among those successfully completed were a textile complex, two oil processing factories, a canned fruit juice factory, soft drinks and chocolate factory, factories for making shoes and dresses, bicycle and truck assembly plants, and a factory for the production of tiles.

In addition, in the industrial sector, there are some small privately-owned industrial units, which in general employ less than fifty workers. These are mainly in areas such as baking, the production of canned fruit and soft drinks, sandals, soap, nails, raincoats; and in entertainment, cinemas and so on.

Productivity of the traditional sector of the economy, such as food crops, livestock, craft work and traditional construction showed a 25 per cent increase between 1958 and 1968. It has been estimated that the production of mining activities, valued at 1,400 million francs in 1959 rose to some 3,000 million in ten years, giving an overall growth of about 4·5 per cent a year, or about 2 per cent a head. 'Real growth has been modest, but it has undoubtedly been higher than that recorded in most West African countries.'[11]

New commercial structures and processes to handle agricultural produce, export and import trade, and the marketing of consumer goods, have been devised as another sector of development. For the commercial sector of a country, unless firmly in the hands of the party-state can be a 'disorganizing' element in the economy by exploiting the people's needs with the aims of personal enrichment. At the level of the P R L, there is need for 'commercial education of the militants with a view to sorting out the cadres who are honest and competent'.[12]

Soon after independence, import and export trade was taken out of the hands of foreign companies and replaced with state corporations, the Guinean External and Internal Trade Agencies. However, in March 1961, these were scrapped as a result of ineffectiveness, and new state companies were set up to handle the business. By then, Guinea had left the franc zone and established its own currency the Guinea franc. In October 1972, a further change was made when the Guinea franc was abolished and replaced by a new unit called the 'syli'.[13] It was part of French neocolonialist policy to continue to tie its former colonies to the metropolitan economy by according them the dubious 'privilege' of remaining within the franc zone, which operated very much for the benefit of France through favourable cooperation agreements and the control of local banks. In opting out of the French franc zone, and in nationalizing banking, Guinea achieved a significant breakthrough in the struggle to prevent French neocolonialist penetration. Within eighteen months of independence, all financial institutions previously in the hands of French capitalists, had been replaced by national institutions, the Central Bank of Guinea (B C R G), the Bank for External Trade (D G C E), the Credit Bank, the Bank for Agricultural Development (B N D A), and the National Insurance Society (S N A).

Economic support from eastern bloc countries and from Ghana made this possible. By 1961, the U S S R had expanded its trade with Guinea by 293 per cent, and had relieved it of most of the export problems faced at independence. China sent agricultural experts to help with the rural collective development campaign. Unlike the companies and governments of the West, which usually demand payment in hard currency, and which charge high rates of interest on loans, the socialist countries are prepared to accept payment in any currency, agree to barter arrangements, and charge a much lower rate of interest. During a visit to Moscow in August 1959, a P D G delegation was promised credits of 140 million roubles about $35 million. This sum was to finance industrial projects under the Three Year Plan, and to provide for the building of the Conakry Polytechnic Institute to take 1,500 students, and the sports stadium in Conakry to seat 25,000 people. There were to be geological surveys for diamonds and gold; and machinery and equipment supplied for mining them. Funds were also to provide agricultural machinery, and technical assistance for the development of Conakry airport and the building of a railway between Conakry and Mamou. Guinea also received credits of $25 million from China, £10 million from Ghana, $10 million from Czechoslovakia, $5 million from Poland, $2.5 million from Hungary, $10 million from East Germany. This in considerable measure helped to tide Guinea over the very difficult few years after independence when Guinea was suddenly cut off from French economic aid, and when Guinea did not enjoy any of the meagre benefit of 'association' with the E E C like other former French colonies.

In the years which followed, and as a result of the Teachers' Plot[14] against the P D G government in November 1961, the Soviet ambassador, Daniel Solod, was expelled from Guinea, and western investment then exceeded eastern bloc assistance. This came to an abrupt end in 1965 with the discovery of the Traders' plot to overthrow the P D G government and establish a capitalist state. It was from that time, at the P D G Eighth Congress, that the party finally committed itself openly to a socialist path of development. By the close of 1970, there were some seventy-one state enterprises, and substantial foreign investment by both East and West in Guinea, most of the agreements on terms very favourable to Guinea.

Economic support from the U S S R, China and eastern bloc countries has necessarily been channelled through state enterprises, and this accelerated the P D G programme of public ownership. The *Comptoir Guinéen de Commerce Extérieur* (C G C E) was set up in July 1959 to handle imports of rice, sugar, cement and some export crops. Shortly afterwards, in May 1960, a similar state enterprise was set up to handle domestic trade. Subsidiary *comptoirs* were then established in each region. In September 1961, both export and import *comptoirs* were abolished. In due course the national enterprise G U I N E X P O R T, with its regional subsidiaries, the *offices de commercialization agricoles* (O C As), and the General Stores handling wholesale and retail trade. In January 1972, Shell, Texaco, Total and Mobil Oil were taken over by the state and merged with existing state enterprises. But still the commercial sector suffered from inefficiency, waste and corruption. In a strong statement, reported in the national newspaper *Horoya* on 11 February 1972, Sékou Touré said: 'We must admit that state trade has been considered by the majority of the state employees as a sector of easy enrichment through theft and malversations.' The P D G still fights a running battle against black marketeers, smugglers, and other economic saboteurs of the anti-people class. This small sector, made maximum use of those Guineans mainly outside the country in order to discredit the P D G government, is expected to dwindle away as economic development matures and as the programme of political education extends.

The building of the necessary infrastructure required for development has involved the stepping up of improvements in the public services, health, education and so on. All are the concern of the entire people, and as such are under national control. Before independence, some $78 million had been invested in Guinea through F I D E S, out of which about $34,360,000 went to Conakry for housing, public health, municipal repairs and improvements to the harbour and airport. Although Guinea, Senegal and Ivory Coast had roughly the same size population, Guinea received between 1947–56 substantially less funds than the other two.

In 1958, as far as communications were concerned, Guinea had the harbour and airport of Conakry, a small port at Benty for handling banana exports, a railway line between Conakry and Kankan which was not in use because of the poor state of the rails, and a small network of roads most of which were untarred. Under the three year and seven year development plans, there was to be an expansion of transport facilities. In 1959, the railway line was reopened under the national railway corporation; and the old rails have gradually been replaced under an agreement signed with China. Between Conakry and the Fria bauxite complex there is now another railway line, reserved for the transport of bauxite and alumina. There is also the Boké railway stretching from the new port of Kamsar to Boké and Sangaredi, some 137 kilometres. This line is used both for the transport of passengers and goods. There are plans for a trans-Guinea railway line to link Conakry with Nzérékoré in the most westerly part of Guinea just north of the Liberian frontier, as part of the Mifergiu project engaged in the mining of iron ore in the region of Mount Nimba. But in common with many other countries, Guinea finds it difficult to make a financial success of the railways, partly because of poor management, but mainly due to rising costs of maintenance and declining passenger and goods traffic. The latter has resulted to some extent from the substantial improvement in roads and airports, and in river transportation.

At independence there were some 8,000 kilometres of roads, of which only 187 kilometres were tarred. By 1970, there were 15,000 kilometres of roads, of which some 1,000 kilometres were tarred. Regarding ports and airport, facilities at Conakry have been greatly improved. The port of Conakry handles most of Guinea's import and export trade, though the new port at Kamsar in the estuary of the Nunez river is expanding rapidly. This port has been constructed to handle the export and import requirements of the Boké bauxite project. Conakry airport has been renovated and the runways improved to take the world's largest aircraft. There are, in addition, some fifteen or so provincial airports served by the national airline, Air Guinée, and increasingly used for domestic travel. River transportation is also being organized to enable more goods and crops to be transported in this way. The maintenance of small boats is cheaper than that of lorries; and barges have also a greater transport capacity.

Similar improvements have been achieved in other public services. For example, in 1958 only some parts of Conakry, Kankan and Labé enjoyed the luxury of a pipeborne water supply. By 1971, pipeborne water had been extended to most regional administrative centres, and has since become available in many other towns and villages. In 1958, there was only one reasonably equipped hospital in Guinea, and one doctor for every 70,000 people. On the completion of the Three Year Plan there were seventeen general hospitals, 160 dispensaries, twenty maternity hospitals and sixty-four health centres. Six schools had been set up to provide training for medical orderlies and nurses; and many Guineans were sent overseas to train as doctors, dentists and pharmacists. Further progress was made during the period of the Seven Year Plan. By 1970, each region had at least one well-equipped hospital; and over 200 dispensaries had been built. In addition, a School of Medicine and a School of Pharmacy had been established which now provide Guinea with a regular supply of qualified doctors and pharmacists. In 1967, an Institute of Traditional Medicine was created which has also helped to improve health services. Obviously, much still remains to be done. The infant mortality rate is high, and adult life expectancy low by standards in the industrialized world, though not in comparison with some other parts of Africa and Asia. More drugs and medical equipment are needed. But again, this problem is being tackled, and it is a problem faced by most countries emerging from colonialism and with widespread endemic diseases associated with tropical regions of the world.

As regards education, a major development zone, there has been a complete break with the colonial past. The *Centre d'Education Révolutionnaire* (C E R) is the name given to schools and colleges from primary to university level. All education is secular, and is integrated into the life of the community. The P D G uses the phrase: 'L'école pour la vie'. Political education is a compulsory subject at all levels, along with training in the practical work of constructing a socialist society. First, there is the *premier cycle de l'enseignement*, the non-specialized period of six years when the child is introduced at the age of seven to the general activities of family and community life, and receives instruction in the usual primary subjects. At the 1968 C N R meeting in Conakry it was decided that first, second and third year pupils should spend half a day each week on productive work or service to the community; and fourth, fifth and sixth year pupils, two and a half days a week. For example, children in rural areas might help with simple agricultural work, and town children with cleaning and tidying paths and buildings. In such ways, children from seven to thirteen years of age gain knowledge and experience of working life. In the second stage, *le deuxième cycle de l'enseignement* which lasts three years for pupils between the ages of thirteen and seventeen, specialization begins. Pupils learn the rudiments of socialist political and economic structures. This is the level of the C E Rs in which 60 per cent of the time is spent on productive work. Students are divided up into working groups according to their particular aptitudes and skills. But in view of the importance attached to agricultural production, emphasis is placed on this area of development work. Each C E R administers its own affairs through a *conseil d'administration* and a political officer with two assistants, one in charge of discipline and the other production. The third educational stage, the *centre d'enseignement révolutionnaire du troisième cycle*, includes all that applies in the second *cycle*, and more besides. It is further specialized in that it trains for the professions and for responsible positions in administration, commerce and industry, and in technological and scientific spheres. Then there is the fourth stage, *l'enseignement supèrieur*, composed of those who have completed courses at second and third level. These students study problems and policies concerning the whole of the nation's development plans, and generally serve the needs of the second and third stage C E Rs. Since they have already received training in either industry or agriculture, these students receiving higher education, are not alienated from the rest of society like so many of their counterparts in capitalist societies.

In Guinea, there is no separation between those who plan and make the machines and those who work them. Socialist revolution requires that everyone shall understand what he does, why, and for whom he is doing it. Each worker in a production unit contributes to the planning of production as well as to the implementation of the plans. 'It is superfluous to add', declared Sékou Touré, 'that in the programme of the C E R, the ideological and political content occupies a key position.'[15] Similarly with the people's army and civic brigades, all soldiers receive in addition to their military training, instruction to enable them to assist in rural development, construction work, engineering and so on. They are technicians and producers, party militants in uniform, who spend part of their time working alongside C E R and production brigades.

Closely associated with the education of Guinea's young people is the P D G youth organization, *Jeunesse de la révolution démocratique africaine* (J R D A). The J R D A complements and enriches C E R training with additional political and civic education as well as sporting and cultural activities, and instruction in practical subjects. It is a mass organization for all young people, irrespective of their ability. There are some 7,200 local J R D A branches, each of them administered through a committee of thirteen members, including at least five girls. Throughout Guinea, the young people of the J R D A meet frequently and regularly to discuss and decide problems concerning their locality and the various aspects of P D G national development plans. There are local meetings, regional conferences and national congresses of youth. For members of the J R D A take an active part in the carrying out of development plans, and also in the actual formulation of P D G policies.

The Guinean nation is itself young, and it is largely administered by young people. The average age of those holding high positions of responsibility is about thirty-five; and under thirty-five years of age for the many thousands who have assumed responsibilities in the P R Ls, C E Rs and other party organizations. 'In Guinea today it can no longer be said that youth means lack of awareness, ignorance or incapacity. Our youth has fully recovered its social role; it is a live and active portion of the community, with the characteristics of its age but intent on acceding to the privilege of culture and acquiring the maturity and political consciousness which will increasingly widen the scope of its militant activity.'[16] Membership of the J R D A, and a satisfactory record of militancy within the organization qualifies a student for entry to higher education even more than excellence in strictly academic subjects. Education is an integral part of the political, social and cultural life of the nation. Students, therefore, are expected to play their part in all aspects of development, from assisting with the implementation of development plans to the administration of their own schools and colleges through elected councils of administration which the councils of teachers are bound to consult.

The Conakry polytechnic, now named after Gamal Abdel Nasser, and the teacher training college at Kankan, together form the national university of Guinea. Here, as in the schools, emphasis is on the teaching of technical and scientific subjects to equip students with the expertise and practical skills needed for economic development plans. Again, students are assessed for their political militancy. All polytechnic students spend a month of each year working in rural areas; and every graduate must spend three months working with a P R L before obtaining employment. Incidentally, all administrators, even to the most senior civil servants and B P N members, are expected to spend periods doing community work.

Sékou Touré does not consider 'intellectuals' as representing an occupation. 'The peasant, the worker, the driver also utilize their intelligence. No man can perform a useful job without using his mind, and therefore his intelligence ... In every physical labour, even the most mechanical and the most humble, there is a minimum of technical qualification, that is, a minimum of creative intellectual activity. That is why one might say that all men are intellectuals.'[17] African 'intellectuals' trained in the educational establishments of capitalist countries are for the most part mentally 'alienated' according to Sékou Touré. There will continue to be alienation as long as higher education remains the privilege of the few. For no people's revolution is possible without the extension of education in the broadest sense to the entire community. The party state of Guinea strives, therefore, to 'transfer to the entire people's class the weapon of science, technology, the practice of production, of manual labour, so as not to train monsters whose heads are not aware of what the hands are doing'.[18] The distinction between manual and non-manual workers has to be abolished.

In recent years there has been a campaign to develop, specially at primary level, eight indigenous languages instead of the three most widely spoken, Mandinka, Fula and Susa. French is taught as a subject from the third year in school. At secondary level, pupils are expected to learn another language in addition to their local language and French. In 1972, a National Academy of Languages was created with help from UNESCO to develop national languages, and to produce manuals and other aids, and to evolve new teaching methods. Closely connected with the work of the Academy is, of course, the adult literacy programme which is central to the PDG's objective of extending educational opportunities to everyone.

As had been shown, popular revolution for the PDG embraces not only political and economic matters but the social and cultural life of the people. All are indeed part of the cultural revolution which is needed for thorough decolonization and the recovery of African 'authenticity', or as some prefer to call it, the 'African personality'. The peoples of Africa collectively and resolutely contribute the values and the creative genius of Africa's cultural heritage to the world's moral and material wealth. For the cultural revolution which Sékou Touré envisages is not concerned with racialist and reactionary notions such as négritude but with the actual making of revolution. In his words: 'There is no other abode for African culture, for the African man as well as for the African people than that of the struggle for liberation, unification and rehabilitation.'[19] The word 're-habilitation' covers every aspect of man's development in society, but as always in P D G ideology, it is given a thoroughly political content, being specifically concerned with the assertion of Africa's dignity, freedom and unity. The positive role played by revolutionary culture in the life of the people is, therefore, the total mobilization of the creative energies of the entire people. There is no place for individuals and egoism. Sport, art, music, drama, and all that contributes to the mental and physical well-being of the people is collectively developed and enjoyed. 'The will of our people is to give a national, African, universal, progressive content to education and to culture.'[20] Everything deemed 'positive' in the culture of foreign countries can be absorbed, but only to enrich Africa's own cultural heritage. Authenticity, dignity, personality, these are the three guiding principles of P D G cultural policy which, as an inseparable part of the party's political programme aims to achieve the fullest possible human development.

Physical training and recreation are organized through party structures from P R L to national level. P R L football and basketball teams, for instance, compete with federation and national teams. Athletics, boxing, swimming, and other sports are encouraged through the construction of sports grounds throughout Guinea; and Guinean sportsmen and women are making a notable impact in African and in world competitions.

Similarly with art, drama, music and dancing, Guineans are acquiring an international reputation. The Guinean national ballet, created in 1959, performs world-wide and is in much demand. Like other artistic production, it is regarded as a social activity and therefore the collective property of the people, an element in their social development. The national ballet bears no-one's name, and there are no stars.

Drama groups, artists, craftsmen, musicians, all are helped by the party and compete regularly in local and national festivals. Each year there is an arts festival lasting two weeks, held in the great People's Palace in Conakry, built with Chinese help during the period of the Three Year Plan. Many foreign delegations attend, and medals are awarded to the best groups. Once again, emphasis is on political themes. All are expected to be fully committed to party ideology and the rejection of such bourgeois concepts as 'art for art's sake'. For just as there is no distinction made between manual and non-manual worker, so also there is no separation recognized between cultural, political, economic and social activities. All are part of the harmonious, complete revolutionary contributing his productivity for the continued development and constant improvement of mankind.

In this connection, the role of women in the Guinean revolution is of special interest. In many traditional African societies, matriarchy conferred on women a paramount social and even political role. But during the colonial period a reversal of the traditional order took place when the African peoples suffered degradation and indignity. The emancipation of women is, therefore, considered by the PDG as part of the decolonization and development process. The party considers that in bourgeois societies where there is a sharply divided social structure, the position of women is blurred by class considerations and interests. But in societies where the community relations of a subsistence economy have not been fundamentally altered, social classes are not always distinct, and the physical groups of young and old, men and woman have a considerable influence on social relations. They are responsible for the growth of several forms of social organization due to the part which each plays in production processes. The forms of organizations are often very different in the various societies, but all without exception help to strengthen social harmony and solidarity to develop community life, and to consolidate its internal balance. Matriarchial forms of organization show that there was no discrimination against women in large areas of African traditional society. However, the widespread practice of polygamy, especially during the colonial period, did raise the question of women's social equality. It became yet another means through which Africans suffered exploitation and oppression. 'This is why we say that the human condition of the woman was, and in many cases still is, that of the slave of a slave.'[21]

Women were in the forefront of the independence struggle in Guinea, a shining example being Aïssata Mafory Bangoura. She and the women of Guinea generally, both before and after independence, have played a full part not only in politics, but in every aspect of national reconstruction. For the P D G insists on the absolute equality of women. The social condition of women is directly linked to the importance of the role that the people play in the exercise of national sovereignty. In other words, the more sovereignty and freedom a people enjoys, and the more effectively it observes and enforces the principles of equality, the better are the living conditions of women in that society.

'The unjust practices engendered by the subjection of woman to man were linked to a given economic predicament and a false social organization.'[22] In spite of measures taken by the P D G, some of these practices continue to debase women, but the struggle to eradicate the last vestiges of them continues. Polygamy was abolished in 1968. The way in which the P D G was able to win acceptance for the abolition of this very entrenched custom was typical of the party's methodology. The political bureau despatched its members to the regions to explain the reasons for the party's decision, and to seek approval. They held meetings and listened as the people expressed their opinions. Many argued vehemently in favour of retaining polygamy since it was a traditional and religious custom. The P D G agreed that the customs of the people must be respected. However, the P D G defined the word 'custom' as meaning the permanent tendency of a people towards progress. It is the expression of justice, liberty, social progress and equality. This is the meaning of 'custom', according to the P D G, and as such it belongs to all societies. The people were given the philosophical and practical reasons for the abolition of polygamy. It was explained to them that in order to build a nation, the values belonging to the entire people must be respected and promoted. Therefore each region, each sector of the population must be prepared to abandon practices which militate against society as a whole and obstruct the building of national unity. The people were convinced by the arguments and accepted the proposal.

By that time, the ground had been well prepared. There had been a remarkable expansion in womens' education. In 1958, only about 4 per cent of girls of school age were in school. The percentage rose to 20 per cent in 1967; and in 1971, some 11 per cent of students in the Conakry polytechnic were women. By 1973, over twenty of the seventy-five members of the National Assembly were women. The women of Guinea are free to participate actively on equal terms with men in discussion and decision making on all issues of communal, regional and national life; and there is no occupation or position of responsibility which is not open to them. For the principle of equality between men and women is generally accepted in Guinea.

The P D G are under no illusion about the difficulties still standing in the way of their development policies. But they are confident of being able to maintain uninterrupted progress. This is because the development programme is not something imposed on the people. It represents what the people themselves have decided, and they themselves are implementing it of their own free will. In 1959, a journalist[23] visiting Guinea reported that he had seen people, entirely voluntarily and without pay, working on Sundays to build roads and schools. This spirit still holds. The masses respond with enthusiasm to appeals to work harder. Not only is there genuine participation at every level in the planning and implementation of development, but there is a readiness to defend their revolutionary gains. The world saw this clearly at the time of the November 1970 invasion, when against seemingly impossible odds, the people of Guinea succeeded in beating off both an air and sea attack, and also an attempted coup by reactionary elements within Guinea. In spite of many other attempts by those inside and outside Guinea wishing to bring down the P D G government, there is no doubt that the people generally support what Sékou Touré calls 'the revolutionary line' which they themselves have formulated, and which they are free to change or adapt. The collective leadership of the P D G are servants of the party and not its masters.

In 1959, when Sékou Touré was on one of his regular tours of the country to meet the people and to discuss local problems with them, he constantly reminded them that independence was only a means to the political, social and economic development of the people. This development, he said, must be guided by three basic principles. First, there must be liberty, and he talked of the liberation of the spirit and the removal of the 'colonial complex'. Secondly, there must be true democracy, meaning that all must take part in development planning and in development work. Thirdly, that there must be social justice, and no divisions in society. The first and second principles of development have been well and truly carried out. The spirit of the people of Guinea is certainly liberated. There is the fullest participation of the entire people at all levels in their own development. The third principle is only partially achieved. There can be said to be social justice in that the exploitation of one person by another is not tolerated. But there are still elements within Guinean society which come within the category of the anti-people class; and in this sense there is not yet developed the collective, communal society at which the people aim. This will take time to achieve. So also will the economic improvement which the P D G plans through the full development of Guinea's natural resources and human potential. But the foundations are laid. The people are on course, and vigilant.

Sékou Touré combines in himself the qualities of the ideal P D G militant. He is first and foremost a political man, a revolutionary activist who has dedicated his life to the service of the people. He is a man of immense courage and great humility, a skilled party worker, teacher, administrator, philosopher and writer. For him, reality and not philosophical theories are the guide to thought and action. The first twenty lines of a poem written by him in February 1975 called 'The Choice of the People' provides an appropriate postscript to the attempt in this chapter to summarize the P D G's programme of development.

Every regime has its morale
And the system of education
Of the ruling class
Every regime has its social base
And the system of government
Of the ruling class.
Every regime has its law
And the system of coercion
And dictatorship of the ruling class.
Every regime has its economy
And its mode of production
In conformity with the interests of the ruling class.

The people of Guinea have made a choice!
They have chosen the Revolution which belongs to all.

They have chosen Africa,
Its history and its true values,
They have chosen suffering humanity
And its objectives of freedom
Of progress and justice.
They have thus made a good choice.[24]

8

THE ANTI-GUINEA PLOT

In July 1977, the PDG found it necessary to publish *La Révolution Guineénne répond à ses détracteurs*,[1] a fully-documented reply to yet another campaign launched in the West against the PDG government. It followed the publication in France of a book, *Prison d'Afrique*, said to have been written by a Frenchman of Guinean nationality, Jean Paul Alata; and articles in the French newspapers *Le Matin* and *Le Monde*, publicising accusations of dictatorship and the suppression of human rights in Guinea, made by expatriate Guineans, notable among them being a certain James Soumah. The anti-Guinea campaign, apparently supported by the French Socialist Party (PSF) contained, according to the PDG, all the same basic elements of the anti-Guinea plot which the PDG maintains has existed since 1958, the purpose being to overthrow the PDG government in order to recolonize Guinea through neo-colonialism. Involved had been the misnamed Front for the Liberation of Guinea (FLING), consisting of Guineans living mainly in France, Ivory Coast, and Senegal; imperialists and neocolonialists wishing to see a change of government in Guinea to allow the replacement of socialist planning by capitalist policies, and the safeguarding of NATO strategic interests in the area of West Africa; elements of the indigenous anti-people class; and finally, Senghor and Boigny and their supporters, who have never approved of Sékou Touré and the PDG for the 'No' vote in 1958, and for so frequently obstructing francophone designs in Africa. The purpose of the 1977 onslaught by these combined forces appeared to the PDG to be to prepare international opinion for a further armed aggression against Guinea.

In an introductory section to the P D G's reply to its detractors, members of the political bureau of the central committee, Damantang Camara and Mamadi Keita, accused the P S F under the leadership of François Mittérand of serving the interests of a section of the French bourgeoisie and international capitalism which were seeking to exploit Guinea's resources as part of a general imperialist strategy to neo-colonize the whole of Africa. The P S F is referred to as a 'fifth column' among democratic forces in France. There follows, in the P D G publication, the text of a speech by Sékou Touré at a mass meeting on 10 June 1977 in the People's Palace in Conakry. In this address, Sékou Touré dealt one by one with the various accusations levelled against Guinea by the P S F, and taken up by Amnesty International and the New York-based League of Human Rights. He analysed the reasons behind the offensive, and exposed the true identity of those whose evidence had been accepted. He revealed that Alata was among those who took part in the invasion of Guinea on 22 November 1970. He was captured by Guinean forces and imprisoned for a time as a war criminal. But his life was spared, and he was released on the special intervention of the French president. As for Soumah, he was reported by *Le Monde* to be an ex-minister in the Guinean government, who had been imprisoned for six months without trial. In fact, he had never been a member of the Guinea government, and had not been imprisoned in Guinea. He was known in Conakry by the name of 'Yemi'. He had failed at the École de Fotoba, and had abandoned his studies to become a fisherman. He found his way to Dakar and then to France in 1952, where he enrolled in a law school in Toulouse after marrying the daughter of a French lawyer. After six years of study he failed to qualify, but returned to Guinea in 1958 with a bogus diploma. Not having a genuine qualification, he failed to get work and eventually, was sent to a re-education centre at Ratoma. After a short time, he fled to Dakar and from there to France where he claimed he had escaped from a 'concentration camp'.

A major argument used by Guinea's detractors, is the existence of considerable numbers of Guineans who evidently prefer to live outside the country. These are the 'exiles' who, according to media sources hostile to the P D G, number about one and a half million, and who fear to return. Yet the vast majority of these Guineans are no more refugees than the many thousands of other Africans who have emigrated from their home countries to work in other states. Many members of the Foulah and Susu peoples, with a long tradition of private trading, did not like the nationalization and cooperative policies of the P D G. They therefore went to live in Ivory Coast, Liberia, Senegal and Sierra Leone, crossing the artificial frontiers of colonialism. These people might possibly be termed 'economic refugees', but they are proud to be Guinean and take no part in subversive plots against the P D G. At the time of the 1970 invasion, these Guinean nationals demonstrated their support for Sékou Touré and the people of Guinea in no uncertain way. In Freetown, for example, some 6,000 Guineans took to the streets to denounce the invaders and to declare their support for the people of Guinea.

While the role of a minority sector of expatriate Guineans in plots to overthrow the P D G is clear, that of the P S F in 1977, can only be understood within the context of the general offensive of reactionary forces against the African people. Sékou Touré and the P D'G are conscious of a continuous struggle by counter-revolutionaries to reconquer Africa for capitalism and the international bourgeoisie. The Guinean revolution, because it is an obstacle in the way of imperialist aggression, is therefore under constant threat. Again and again, charges are made in the West that the people of Guinea are suffering under a dictatorship, and that there are secret trials and executions. Both these charges are demonstrably false. In Guinea, popular power is a reality; and on the question of justice, no-one in Guinea is sentenced to death or imprisonment in secret. Offenders are tried openly, and by the people. There is a free legal service, and judges are elected by the people.

It is unfashionable to talk in terms of 'conspiracy', but it is understandable that the P D G refers to a 'permanent plot'. For there does appear to have been a campaign to discredit and isolate Guinea. On each occasion that there has been an actual attempt to overthrow the P D G, the same hostile foreign and indigenous elements have been involved, apparently condoned by Boigny and Senghor, and foreign intelligence organizations. While few would maintain that all these counter-revolutionary elements actually get together and plot, it seems they have all been involved to some degree in the preparing and carrying out of subversion against Guinea. As Sékou Touré declared in 1977, in the midst of the P S F-Alata-Soumah affair, when he confidently predicted the victory of the Guinean people: 'They don't know us. But we know them.'

At a session of the C N R in Conakry 15–18 July 1977, he listed the different categories of Guineans living outside the country, and stated the conditions on which they could return to help in the work of development. It is instructive to note how the P D G regards them since it helps in the understanding of why many Guineans continue to live abroad, and why some of them are prepared to assist imperialists and neocolonialists in trying to overthrow by force the popularly-elected P D G government. First, Sékou Touré said, there are those Guineans who have lived aboard since birth and have assumed the mental habits of the countries in which they have been living. These, if they wished to return to Guinea, would be welcomed, and allowance would be made for their different life-style until they reintegrated with the Guinean people. Secondly, there are Guineans who were born and brought up in Guinea, and engaged in business for a time, but who left to live in another African country or in Europe, where they could make more money for themselves. Some had left families behind in Guinea. Others had married foreigners and had families in the countries of their adoption. These businessmen could return if they wished, and certain financial and business guarantees would be given to them to enable them to establish enterprises in Guinea to help speed up the economic development of the country. They were promised exemption from import duties on equipment needed for their businesses, though once the enterprise was established they would be subject to the same conditions as all other national and private enterprises. For example, they would only be able to export through the national export organization. But they would be able to sell their produce for export on the same terms as those who had never left the country. Thirdly, declared Sékou Touré, there are Guineans born and educated in Guinea, who fled after committing subversive acts or engaging in dishonest trading. These persons would be allowed back if they were prepared to make a genuine contribution to the development of the nation. Then there are the so-called intellectuals, bureaucrats and professional people who left Guinea in search of gain, and in the hope that they might one day return after a neocolonialist regime had been installed. Many of these people had taken part in agitation and propaganda campaigns against the Guinean revolution, with a view to isolating it and making it vulnerable to attack. Some, he said, were implacable enemies of the PDG, their hostility going back to pre-independence days; but there were some who might have second thoughts and be prepared to return and make their contribution to the land of their birth. Finally, there are the 'perdus', the lost ones, who live in a manner now banned in Guinea. These are the private practice doctors, lawyers, pharmacists, and others, many of whom have spread lies about Guinea. Some might return, taking advantage of the offer made to rehabilitate them, and then try to make trouble by causing dissension. But even these people would be allowed to return, though special vigilance would have to be exercised. For the PDG was not opening the door to expatriates merely for the sake of opening the door, but only in an attempt to accelerate national economic development.

Critics of the PDG immediately interpreted the offer of amnesty and rehabilitation as a sign of weakness. It surely demonstrates quite the reverse in that it shows the confidence of the people of Guinea in their ability to accept the risk of admitting reactionary elements in their midst, and of harnessing them to help in the work of development.

The PDG has had plenty of experience in handling counter-revolutionary activity. As early as 1959 arms dumps were discovered along Guinea's borders with Ivory Coast and Senegal, evidently to be used by Guinean dissident ex-servicemen in conjunction with local reactionaries consisting of traditional chiefs hoping to regain their lost power; and elements wishing to return Guinea to the French Community. There followed in 1961 the Teachers' Plot, originating in a dispute between the government and the teachers' union over working conditions. In a document setting out the teachers' claims, there was general criticism of some of the policies of the P D G, and in particular the policy of non-alignment. At that time, when the cold war was at its height, most of the African states as they became independent joined the non-aligned movement, not wishing to become involved in the disputes of the superpowers. Students and teachers demonstrated in Conakry with placards demanding more radical policies and a clear commitment to the socialist world. The Russian ambassador, Daniel Semyonovitch Solod, who was accused of complicity, was expelled, and for a short time relations between the U S S R and Guinea were very strained.

In those early years of Guinea's independence, both East and West competed for Guinea's friendship. It is necessary, therefore, to analyse the anti-Guinea plot within the context of cold war politics and ideologies. Initially, because of the circumstances of Guinea's independence, and the immediate help given by socialist countries, it was thought by some that Guinea might become a West African 'Cuba'. But to many political observers, the position was by no means clear-cut in spite of the known progressive policies of the P D G. In October and November 1959, Sékou Touré visited the U S A, Britain and West Germany, as well as the U S S R and Czechoslovakia. He arrived in Washington on 26 October 1959, to be welcomed by President Eisenhower and a crowd of some 76,000. The stand made by Guinea in the 1958 French referendum had received wide publicity in the American press, and great admiration was felt for the young leader of Africa's newest independent state. Sékou Touré spent ten days visiting various parts of the U S A, including the Olin-Mathieson Corporation in Virginia, which had extensive bauxite interests in Guinea.

Clearly, the welcome given to Sékou Touré in the U S A was not disinterested. American big business recognized great opportunities with the ending of colonial rule in large areas of Africa, especially in territories which had rich mineral resources. Claiming to have a fellow feeling for colonial peoples since America also had once been colonized, the U S A saw a way of making economic gains in Africa by appearing in the role of a sympathetic friend at a time when European powers were unpopular as colonizers, and when the newly-independent states were keen to establish new trading patterns. Sékou Touré told Washington's press club that the purpose of his visit to the U S A was to obtain an adaptation and orientation of U S policy to promote the rapid emancipation of Africa. 'Africa has great moral and spiritual values, and respect of man for man', he said. 'What she lacks are the techniques for development.' But his most important speech was made before the U N General Assembly in New York. There he denounced colonialism and accused 'certain governments' of adopting a 'policy of puppets', and of exercising a paternalism which 'has taken from certain African leaders their sense of dignity and responsibility'. Listening on that occasion was Boigny. Neither he nor the members of the French delegation joined in the clapping at the end of Sékou Touré's speech. On the East–West situation, Sékou Touré with customary bluntness said the two power blocs should be asked: 'Yes or No, are you for the liberation of Africa?' Their answers would determine the attitude of Africa towards them. A cultural agreement was signed between the U S A and Guinea providing for the exchange of professors, specialists and so on; and also an agreement for an American trade mission to visit Guinea.

After leaving the U S A, Sékou Touré and his party visited London, Bonn, Moscow and Prague. At the end of the U K visit, a communique was issued referring in vague terms to technical and cultural cooperation. Much the same happened in Germany. Yet sections of the French press resented even that degree of interest being shown in Guinea. The newspaper *L'Aurore* described Sékou Touré as a 'dictator', and declared that the French could not help feeling hurt by the attention paid to him by Eisenhower, Macmillan and Adenauer.

The visits to Moscow and Prague were in a different category. The USSR had already provided a £12 million loan to Guinea and Sékou Touré and his party were enthusiastically welcomed in Moscow. A special Ilyushin-18 aircraft had been sent to Frankfurt to fetch them. They spent eight days in the Soviet Union during which agreements were signed providing among other things for an exchange of students, and for cooperation in training and cultural activities. Sékou Touré declared that he was glad to be in the USSR, and specially so since he had read in many newspapers in the West that he had spent his youth there studying Marxism!

Sékou Touré paid a second visit to the USSR in September 1960. In the same year he also visited China. Like the USSR, China had been among the first to recognize the independent state of Guinea and to render economic assistance, particularly in the agricultural sphere. He received a great welcome in Peking where he had long discussions with Chou En-Lai and Mao Tse-Tung. Sékou Touré said that he was 'quite overwhelmed' by the mass demonstrations which greeted him everywhere he went. Friendship and trade agreements were signed, and China made Guinea a loan of 100 million roubles on terms more favourable than the 140 million roubles granted by the USSR in 1959. The Chinese loan was free of interest, whereas the USSR charged 2·5 per cent although this was far less than the rates customarily charged by capitalist countries of the West. In addition, the Chinese experts sent to help development plans in Guinea were to be paid the same as equivalent Guinean officials. This again was a departure from other foreign practice, their experts being paid higher expatriate salaries. In a speech at a dinner given in his honour, Sékou Touré declared: 'We can assure you that we Africans know where truth is to be found; for Africans know that you had to fight against the same foes they are now fighting. They know that the great victory you have won is their victory too.' Sékou Touré, like other African leaders visiting China, saw that there was much in the Chinese revolutionary experience which could be applied to Africa.

In view of the obvious rapport between the people of Guinea and the peoples of socialist countries, the apparent change in the political atmosphere in Guinea as a result of the Teachers' Plot in 1961 appeared all the more remarkable. But there is never a power vacuum while powerful ideologies compete for spheres of influence. The new American ambassador to Guinea, William Attwood who had arrived in Conakry only three days before the expulsion of the Soviet ambassador, was quick to make the most of the situation. At that time, according to Attwood, the U S A was just waking up to the importance of Africa. 'We in America had barely started discovering Africa, even though more than twenty million Americans were of African descent. The stock image of Africa was, and for the most part still is, a vision of vast jungles populated by cannibals, witch doctors, Mau Mau savages, lions, gorillas, Tarzan, Jane and Dr Schweitzer ... And while we dawdled, the Russians, and to a lesser extent the Chinese, were already getting very busy in Africa.'[2] For six months after Guinea's independence, the U S A sent no ambassador to Conakry for fear of offending de Gaulle. Meanwhile, as Attwood observed, there were by 1961 over a thousand Soviet bloc technicians in Guinea advising and helping with development work. On his last day in the U S A before leaving for Conakry, Attwood described how he was briefed by the C I A, who wished to be informed about Soviet bloc activities. He wrote that as a result of a presidential directive of 29 May, ambassadors were to receive authority to supervise C I A activities in the field. This was to be of significance as further plots against the PDG developed.

Meanwhile, the U S A through ambassador Attwood offered Guinea an 'aid' package designed to bring the country into the western fold. There was to be a dam and power station which would double Guinea's hydro-electric power, the construction of six plants for processing consumer goods; a turbine and generator to meet Conakry's power requirements; a vocational training programme for Guinean workers; equipment and teachers for a public administration school; the construction and staffing of a teacher training institute; scholarships for Guinean students to study in the USA; technical assistance for increasing corn and rice production; a commodity import scheme whereby certain US goods could be bought with Guinean francs; and finally, the provision of forty Peace Corps volunteers to assist in education, health and public works. According to Attwood, the package was agreed in full and 'we were now in business'.[3]

As part of the package, the Guinea government declared its intention of joining the International Monetary Fund (IMF); and an investment guarantee agreement was signed with the USA. Attwood was pleased to note that the communist bookstore in Conakry went out of business, and that some French communist teachers who had stayed on after independence began drifting away.

In October 1962, Sékou Touré made a second visit to the USA. President Kennedy promised Guinea more economic aid and assistance in normalizing relations between Guinea and France. Three Guinean ministers remained behind in Washington to work out detailed plans with American government officials. This visit of Sékou Touré's took place just one week before the Cuban missile crisis flared up. The USSR requested landing rights in Conakry for their long-range jet aircraft. The new runway there had been built with Soviet aid. But permission was refused on the grounds of Guinea's policy of positive neutrality. At this point, American influence in Guinea was probably at its height. After that, it began to decline sharply as subversion within Guinea, coupled with a stepping up of capitalist pressures from outside accelerated the radicalization of the PDG.

At the Sixth Congress of the PDG held in Conakry between 27 and 31 December 1962, it became apparent that there were party members who did not support certain basic PDG policies. They said that the party should not meddle with commerce because it lacked the necessary knowledge and experience. They also opposed policies of decentralization, declaring that the masses were insufficiently educated, and that it would be at least ten or fifteen years before powers could be granted to the base. Sékou Touré answered them in the longest speech he had ever made. It lasted almost without pause from 8.30 a.m. to 7.30 p.m. Those who became exhausted were invited to withdraw. But in order to discover the true plot within the party, delegates were asked to write down the names of seventeen persons for the party leadership. A voting paper reveals the class attitude of the voter, and on analysing the votes the 'union of reactionaries' could be clearly discerned. Everyone wrote down the secretary-general's name, but the names of other members of the national leadership were omitted in favour of all those who were later revealed to be fifth columnists. Due note was taken of them.

Between 1961 and 1964, the period of strong western involvement in Guinea, 'malpractices increased', and in the words of Sékou Touré: 'Everything became rotten ... the élite enjoyed riding in cars and building villas.'[4] The party tried to counter the reactionary movement, organizing meetings to assess the reaction of cadres. As a result, Sékou Touré received a mandate to launch the attack. An announcement was made that he would address the nation on Sunday 8 November 1964 in the Conakry stadium. Huge crowds gathered to hear him. This time his speech was short. He denounced the 'emerging bourgeoisie', and the apathy and backsliding of certain sections of the party. Assets acquired fraudulently would be confiscated. The value of those confiscated in Conakry alone was 2,500,000 francs. People whose monthly pay hardly reached 10,000 francs had acquired millions, the origin of which they could not explain.

There is a striking resemblance to Sékou Touré's stadium address of 8 November 1964 and Kwame Nkrumah's famous Dawn Broadcast of 8 April 1961, when he also adopted the technique of going straight to the people when announcing the removal of unsound party members before they sabotaged the party's socialist programme. Both Nkrumah in 1961 and Sékou Touré in 1964 found themselves faced with a national bourgeoisie in close liaison with neocolonialists, and leading party members which had links with them through a common commitment to a capitalist path of development. Many of them had been prominent in the national liberation movement, but had not matured politically since then. In Ghana, the C P P government survived only five more years after the dismissing of the 'old guard' and the firm commitment to socialism. In Guinea, the struggle continues.

Sékou Touré in a press interview in March 1974, referred to the progress of revolution as like a train which is constantly travelling along a line. The phases or stages end and begin at each station. As on a railway journey, at each station certain passengers leave the train. They have reached their destination in that they have gone as far as they intended. Others, wishing to progress farther, take their place. A condition for the success of the revolution is that it continues to make progress, gathering speed as it goes along.[5]

Between the years 1964 and 1967, national democracy developed in Guinea and assumed a more radical content. This was the period of the socialization of the P D G, leading to popular democracy and the intensification of the struggle against the national bourgeoisie. It was during this period that the Traders' Plot was uncovered. This was evidently an attempt by local capitalist elements to overthrow the P D G and install a pro-French government. A French journalist writing in *Le Monde*[6] admitted French involvement. The French government did not deny it, and their ambassador in Conakry was told to leave. As on other occasions when plots have been discovered, the P D G found evidence of the involvement of the Senegal and Ivory Coast governments in allowing expatriate Guineans and mercenaries to train and organize in their territories.

At the Eighth Congress of the P D G in October 1967, the building of socialism was officially proclaimed as the objective of the party; and it followed from a resolution adopted at this Congress that the P R Ls were established. From then onwards the struggle grew fiercer. On 2 August 1968, the 'radical revolution' was launched, and 'within the party, counter-revolution started to organize itself ... its aim being to take over power, thanks to the aggression prepared jointly with counter-revolution from abroad'.[7]

The year 1969 saw the discovery of a plot within the army led by the Chief of Staff, Colonel Kaman Diaby, in collaboration with a government minister, Fodebo Keita. After that, measures were introduced to speed up the process of integrating the army more closely with the people through political education and participation in agricultural and other production tasks. In October 1969, all soldiers became civil servants and could move or be transferred to any section of the public service. At the same time, steps were taken to increase the size of the militia. But the crucial testing time was still to come.

This began during the night of 22 November 1970, when Guinea was invaded by Portuguese and mercenary forces based in Guinea-Bissau, in collusion with Guinean traitors both inside and outside the country. It was the culmination of a chronology of plots which had occured at intervals ever since independence. All the ingredients of former attempts to destroy the P D G government were there: fifth columnists, expatriate Guineans supported by French intelligence and the governments of Senegal and Ivory Coast. But this time there was an additional factor, the Portuguese and mercenary troops serving the interests of N A T O powers. For some months before the attack, Sékou Touré had warned of the build-up of hostile forces in Senegal and Ivory Coast, and of military preparations in Guinea-Bissau which could only be intended for an assault on Guinea in a desperate attempt to stop the P D G's support for the P A I G C liberation movement. So that when the actual assault was made, the people of Guinea were prepared, though they did not know precisely when the attack would be made.

Under cover of darkness and a thick sea mist, hundreds of troops were disembarked from Portuguese warships at various points along the Conakry coast during the early hours of 22 November 1970. Their immediate targets were the presidential residence, army barracks, radio station, power station, airport, and the headquarters in Conakry of the P A I G C. Many of Guinea's regular troops were in the interior doing agricultural work, and therefore the brunt of the attack was borne by the militia and the civilian population, over 300 of whom were killed. Belle Vue, a government guesthouse where Nkrumah stayed for a few weeks when he arrived in Conakry in March 1966, was burned down. Amilcar Cabral's house was also attacked, but he was out of the country. The circumstances of the attempt to kill Cabral recall the 1969 assassination of Eduardo Mondlane, the founder of F R E L I M O, the liberation movement then fighting to free Mozambique from Portuguese colonial rule. The hand of the Portuguese secret police was widely accepted as being implicated in his murder. The assassination of Cabral in Conakry on 21 January 1973, by agents of Portuguese colonialism may be seen as a postscript to the 1970 invasion of Guinea when that attempt to eliminate him failed.

Within minutes of the opening of the naval bombardment of Conakry, members of the people's army and militia, workers, party militants and even schoolboys were in the streets, and along the shores, fighting the invaders with any weapon they could lay their hands on. Soon they were joined by contingents from the regions. The invaders were prevented from seizing key points including the radio station and the airport, though they did succeed in freeing some prisoners being held by the Guinea government. Within a short time, Sékou Touré was broadcasting to the people informing them of how the battle was going, and proclaiming that Guineans would defend themselves 'to the last drop of blood'. He called upon 'all those who are aware of national dignity and the historic interest of Africa to rise up together with courage and confidence to crush the enemy decisively ... we know that reactionary forces all over the world are speculating over the future of Guinea and the bonds of neo-colonialism. These enemies of Africa are mistaken. They will always be mistaken. Guinea will never come under the domination of neocolonialism.' He warned against traitors inside the country, and called on every P D G militant to take up the arms issued to them in order to crush the mercenaries: 'Guinea must in effect become the grave of imperialism.'

As the fighting continued in and around Conakry, and attacks were launched inland from bases in Senegal and

Ivory Coast, it became clear that the invasion was definitely planned to coincide with an internal uprising. Captured mercenaries, known as 'commandos of death', told how they had each been given a large sum of escudos and informed they would receive support from dissidents in Conakry who would be clearly identifiable by their green armbands. By evening, Conakry radio reported the arrival of PDG reinforcements from Labé, Kankan, Nzérékoré and Kissidougou. Other comrades in arms were on their way from Boké, Forecariah, Fria, Dubreka, Boffa and Kindia. 'Our people have taken up arms and are now on the offensive. The struggle is now general. The defence of the nation must be a matter of life and death for us. Comrades, on with the struggle. We have no better defenders than ourselves.' At 22.30 hours, all strategic points in Conakry were held by the people. From then onwards, although there were further landings of mercenaries and fighting went on during the next day and night, the battle was won. The new landings were made not to consolidate the aggression, but in a desperate bid to secure the retreat of groups of mercenaries which had been cut off by the revolutionary forces. Some of them managed to re-embark into the Portuguese warships. But when the ships finally departed, many of the invaders were left behind and were gradually forced to surrender.

There then began the protracted task of making a full examination of the whole experience so that the correct lessons could be learned from it and appropriate measures taken to prevent a recurrence. Although in the past there was scepticism expressed, particularly in Ivory Coast and Senegal, about the genuineness of the plotting which the PDG often claimed threatened the people of Guinea, no-one could deny the reality of the 22 November 1970 invasion. The OERS states, Senegal, Mauritania and Mali, immediately adopted a resolution calling for 'une sanction exemplaire' against the mercenaries. Within forty-eight hours, the UN Security Council passed a resolution declaring the aggression a threat to peace and security, and decided to send a fact-finding mission to Guinea.

The UN mission, consisting of delegates from Zambia,

Nepal, Columbia, Poland and Finland, confirmed on 4 December 1970 that Portuguese armed forces, commanded by white Portuguese officers, took part in the invasion. Between 350 and 400 troops made the landing, the report said, from ships manned by predominantly white Portuguese, and commanded by white Portuguese officers. The Portuguese troops who took part in the actual landing at Conakry were mainly Africans from 'Portuguese' Guinea; and they were accompanied by a contingent of Guinean dissidents trained and armed in the Portuguese-ruled territory. The U N mission confirmed that the naval force consisted of two troop-carrying ships, and three or four patrol ships. The troops wore uniforms resembling those used by the Guinean army, and were armed with bazookas and mortars in addition to the usual infantry weapons. Portuguese, mercenaries, hostile foreign intelligence organizations were all proved to have been involved with expatriate Guineans based mainly in Ivory Coast and Senegal, in collusion with local quislings.

Many countries responded to Sékou Touré's appeal for help without waiting for the outcome of the U N fact-finding mission. Offers of aid poured into Conakry. China, the U S S R and countries of the eastern bloc, as well as progressive parties and organizations throughout the world, at once condemned the invasion and offered to help Guinea in its heroic struggle. China informed Sékou Touré that the sum of £800,000 had been made immediately available. The secretary-general of the O A U reported that the forty-one member states expressed 'complete solidarity' and were considering concerted action. Nigeria and Sierra Leone offered to put their armies at Guinea's disposal. Egypt offered airborne troops. Tanzania supplied generous financial help. Zambia sent an envoy to find out how the people of Zambia could be of assistance. In Somalia, a register was opened for volunteers willing to fight in Guinea. Yugoslavia, Libya and Algeria sent arms and ammunition. Uganda, then under the presidency of Milton Obote, sent a message of support and promised aid.

In striking contrast was the attitude of governments

committed to the West. Ivory Coast, for example, officially condemned the aggression, but nevertheless closed Abidjan university when the students demonstrated in support of Guinea. The Guinea government thereupon shouldered complete responsibility for the education of the dismissed students by offering them scholarships to continue their education in the country of their choice.

At a special O A U meeting of African foreign ministers in Lagos on 9 December 1970, a resolution was passed condemning the invasion of Guinea. There was much rhetoric and righteous indignation. But the fact remained, the O A U could do little more than render moral support to Guinea. There was no effective machinery even for emergency meetings to be summoned within a few days of a crisis. Small arms did arrive in Conakry from member states, but were too late to be effective. If the invasion had been on a bolder scale it might have succeeded in spite of the stubborn resistance of the Guinean people. The dangers of the continuing disunity of Africa had once again been clearly demonstrated. 'It is only where small states exist that it is possible by landing a few thousand marines or by financing a mercenary force, to secure a decisive result.'[8] So said Nkrumah. He and Sékou Touré were in full agreement on the urgent need for the unification of Africa. 'We have before us not only an opportunity but a historic duty. It is in our hands to join our strength, taking sustenance from our diversity, honouring our rich and varied traditions and culture, but acting together for the protection and benefit of us all.'[9]

Nkrumah was in Conakry at the time of the invasion, and it is not difficult to imagine what he thought as he witnessed the aggression and helped to organize the defence of the area where he was living. He had just written two books particularly relevant to Guinea's situation. The first was the *Handbook of Revolutionary Warfare: A guide to the armed phase of the African Revolution*;[10] and the second was *Class Struggle in Africa*,[11] in both of which he analysed the various aspects of the African revolutionary struggle and exposed the close links between indigenous reactionaries and neocolonialists. The invasion of Guinea bore out his thesis of class struggle in Africa and the need for revolutionary preparedness to defeat the forces of counter-revolution which included the indigenous bourgeoisie, imperialist governments and neocolonialists, and also the puppet governments of African states. The latter were clearly recognizable in their immediate reaction to news of the invasion of Guinea. Their leaders, out of habit, reached for their telephones to suggest a conference. While the people of progressive countries reached for their guns and offered military and financial help. They did so, knowing that an attack on one was an attack on all of them.

In a message to the O A U ministerial council meeting in Lagos, Sékou Touré called for an 'offensive' to liberate remaining parts of Africa still under foreign domination: 'The African states must not wait for the imperialists to take a new initiative to organize another attack. This is the time for the African countries to launch an offensive. In their fight for the rapid liberation of Africa they have nothing to lose apart from the chains of slavery still binding some of our African brothers.' Cabral, secretary-general of the P A I G C, endorsed Sékou Touré's appeal: 'I feel certain,' he said, 'that the whole of Africa will know how to take the necessary measures to strengthen its defensive capacity against imperialism, and also to increase the concrete moral and political aid to the peoples who are still struggling for their national liberation.'[12] He added: 'I want to stress that I am certain that the forces of anti-colonialism in the world, all the socialist countries and the international workers' movement will draw the necessary conclusions from all this to strengthen everything leading to greater unity in the anti-imperialist camp.' He knew that Portugal had attempted to overthrow the P D G government because of its assistance to the P A I G C, and that N A T O support for Portugal had evidently been assured. It was significant that the U S A, Britain, France and Spain all abstained from voting in the U N Security Council resolution condemning Portugal. The strategic importance of the Azores, Guinea-Bissau, the Cape Verde Islands, and the whole west African coastline formed an integral part of the Atlantic defences of the West. As soon as the aggression began, the Guinea government had appealed to the Security Council for help. The U N representative in Conakry had witnessed the invasion and had sent a report to the United Nations. Despite this, the Security Council only sent a mission of inquiry. 'As far as I am concerned,' said Sékou Touré to a Nigerian delegation which arrived in Conakry to arrange military help, 'I think the African countries should learn this basic lesson. They must understand that we alone are responsible for our sovereignty; and that it is only by our stand, our struggle and our unity that we can safeguard Africa's dignity.'[13]

It was abundantly clear that the majority of the people of Guinea supported the P D G and had no wish to be 'liberated' by F L I N G or any other force. It could only then be the small minority of exploiters, capitalists or feudalists who wished to be freed by counter-revolutionary forces. Revolutionary workers and peasants had met armed counter-revolution. It was class struggle at its peak, the culmination of a process accelerated by long-standing contradictions within Guinea society, which had been sharpened by the entry of multinational companies. The P D G had called on the masses to accept the challenge, and their response had shown their revolutionary preparedness.

In the aftermath of the invasion, about a hundred West Germans were deported and ambassador Joachim-Christian Lanke was told to leave. The P D G was convinced of West German involvement in the aggression. Some West German nationals had been taken prisoner by the revolutionary forces while the invasion was in progress. The P D G also claimed that the German television network had prepared a programme to be shown later on the day of the invasion, when it was confidently expected that the operation had been a complete success; thereby proving prior knowledge of the aggression. The U S A, Britain and France were all suspected of undercover encouragement of the invaders, along with the old leadership in Ivory Coast and Senegal. But in condemning external collusion, Sékou Touré and the P D G consistently refused, as always, to accuse peoples. Their quarrel is always with individuals and systems, never with peoples.

External aggressors had revealed themselves for all to see. Not so easy to discover were the internal accomplices, those who did not actually surface at the time of the invasion, but who would certainly have done so had the aggression shown any sign of success. Compared with some other African countries, Guinea hardly has a class which can be called 'capitalist'. But that does not mean that it lacks traders, bureaucrats and ambitious people who aspire to become capitalists. The desire of those wishing to become capitalists is no less strong than the determination of those who are already capitalists to remain so. Therefore, although it would be incorrect to maintain the existence in Guinea of a bourgeoisie in the generally accepted sense, there are those who have a bourgeois mentality. These are the natural allies of those who traditionally held a privileged position in society, and who hanker after a return to the 'good old days'.

The extent of internal betrayal of the Guinean revolution shocked the people of Guinea as much as it surprised the rest of the world. As investigations proceeded, it became apparent that many of the traitors had occupied very responsible positions. Among them were seventeen government ministers, eight governors, twenty members of the armed forces, forty high level bureaucrats, fifteen top party officials and seven foreigners living in Guinea. There were, in addition, businessmen, technicians and professional and specialist people who had been directly concerned with PDG development planning. Sékou Touré referred to them as 'this unscrupulous bourgeois class ... this rotten social class which goes around crying "economic waste" when it is the author of that waste'.[14] It was, he said, a 'mercantile bourgeoisie, a mercenary bourgeoisie', which had accepted the bribes of imperialism and betrayed the people.

The entire nation was asked to judge the traitors. Revolutionary local authorities and production units in all villages, work sites and enterprises throughout Guinea held special meetings to discuss the invasion, and to decide how the enemies of the nation should be punished. The 210 party sub-branches held extraordinary congresses for the same purpose. Then the thirty party branches and the country's specialized organizations, the National Confederation of

Guinea Workers, the J R D A, the National Women's Organization, and committees of the people's revolutionary army met to discuss the same matters. The prisoners were divided into four categories. First, there were the Portuguese soldiers arrested in Conakry, Gaoual and Koundara; secondly, mercenaries used by Portugal in the attack; thirdly, local accomplices who had been in contact with the Portuguese authorities during the preparation and execution of the attack; and fourthly, foreign accomplices similarly implicated. It was generally agreed by the people's committee that all mercenaries and fifth columnists should suffer the death penalty; and that all foreigners found guilty of direct or indirect participation in the aggression should be imprisoned, and that diplomatic relations with their countries of origin should be broken off. There were local variations in how the recommendations should be carried out, but no disagreement on broad principles. The verdicts of the people's committees were submitted through the various levels of administration and on up to the National Assembly, which transformed itself into a supreme tribunal for the purpose of coordinating the people's judgements. What party in the world, asked the P D G, is capable of saying to entire people, 'judge these cases, give your verdicts'? Yet the P D G did just that.

In retrospect, Sékou Touré considered the whole experience of 22 November 1970 had served a valuable purpose in galvanizing the energies of the Guinean people. It was, he said, 'one of those sublime moments of exaltation and patriotism ... the affirmation of collective dignity'.[15] The defeat of the invaders had shown Africa and the world the maturity of the African people and their ability to defend their sovereignty and dignity. Guineans had learned not to relax vigilance. They had been ashamed, he said, of the extent of internal treachery and were determined that such a disgrace must not occur again: 'The dismantling and liquidation of the imperialist fifth column, directly carried out by the people themselves, is a historical lesson which confirms the invincibility of an organized and educated people ... that is why Africa as a whole, as well as all the democratic organizations of the world hailed the victory of the Guinean people, as a victory of the progressive forces of the world. And we must always stand to score new victories at the expense of imperialism and colonialism as a contribution of the people of Guinea to the progress of the forces of world revolution.'[16]

Investigations into every aspect of the events of November 1970 proceeded throughout 1971. Mass meetings were held in every region of Guinea to 'understand the lessons' of the experience. No attempt was made to hide any of the findings of the people's inquiries, or of the measures taken as a result of them. The outcome was a more thorough and better definition of people's power, a deeper radicalization of the revolution leading to the phase of the party-state.

But by 1973, Sékou Touré was again warning the people: 'Comrades, imperialism is still at war against us, and we carry out the same war against Senghor and Houphouët, traitors to Africa and servile agents of imperialism.' The PDG government had received reports of further preparations being made against Guinea, particularly in Senegal. As always, Sékou Touré distinguished between Senghor, whom he described as 'an accident of Africa', and the people of Senegal: 'The Senegalese people can count on the confidence, the admiration and the solidarity of the militant people of Guinea.'[17] He accused Senghor of spending more than a million dollars on supporting anti-Guineans at a meeting in Lisbon with Portuguese military authorities. In reply to the accusations, Senghor declared that Sékou Touré was inventing plots in order to divert attention from domestic difficulties. Thereupon, Sékou Touré challenged Senghor to agree to a referendum in Senegal and Guinea to find out whether the people wished to get rid of their respective heads of state. While the referendums were held, Sékou Touré and Senghor would remain in another African state.

The PDG also declared at this time, that France was still aiding and abetting subversion against Guinea by sending former Guinean soldiers who had remained in France after 1958, to form anti-Guinean groups in Ivory Coast and Senegal.

Again, in 1974, the P D G was informed that there were some 1,500 mercenaries stationed along the Ivory Coast and Senegal borders. According to the report,[18] there were three warships ready to disembark troops by sea while other land forces created diversions along the frontiers. Guinea complained to the United Nations about the complicity of Senegal and Ivory Coast. Their governments promptly denied Guinea's allegations, and said that if indeed there was a plot it had been planned without their knowledge by dissident Guineans. But before the U N could deal with the matter, Guinea withdrew the complaint and submitted it instead to the O A U, where it has apparently remained unresolved.

Two years later, on 13 May 1976, the 'Foulah plot' was exposed. This was the first time that a plot had been associated with an ethnic group rather than with a class or individuals. In a broadcast made at the time, Sékou Touré denounced 'Foulah racialism'. The plot had evidently originated in the Fouta Djallon region where the Foulahs form the majority of the population. According to statements made by some of the accused, the plan was to replace Sékou Touré by the former Justice minister, Diallo Telli. It was reported that he had confessed, but declared that no violence was intended. The P D G leaders were simply to have been 'detained'. Diallo Telli, who was for some time secretary-general of the O A U, was accused of working for the American intelligence agency, the C I A. He was said to have been recruited by the Liberian ambassador to Guinea. Another Guinean minister, a former Minister of Planning, Alioune Drame, was also declared to have confessed to being involved in the conspiracy. Among other prominent Guineans arrested for complicity were Sy Savane, Inspector-General of State Services, Captain Lamine Kouyaté, commander of the Kindia garrison, and Serkou Silou, a former ambassador to Algeria. But not all the detainees were Foulahs; and there were many Foulahs in the government who strongly denounced the plot. Apart from dissident expatriate Guineans and the many Foulahs implicated, the P D G named France, West Germany, Ivory Coast, Senegal and the U S A as being involved.

The PDG from its foundation has always pursued policies of ethnic integration. Article 45 in the constitution declared that 'any act of racial discrimination as well as all propaganda of a racial or regional character shall be punishable by law'; and on the whole, the bid to end tribalism and regionalism in Guinea has achieved much success. In 1964, Sékou Touré admitted that there was still some way to go: 'Regionalism and racism have not completely disappeared ... Our great victory, however is that the people, in an official manner, can no more believe in regionalism and racism.'[19] The PDG has refused to operate a so-called ethnic arthimetic in either the administration or in development. The party's purpose is to achieve even development throughout the country. It must, therefore, have come as a disappointment to have found large numbers of a particular ethnic sector of the population involved in a plot to overthrow the government. But too much significance should not be attached to the name given to the plot. Thorough examination and analysis by the party of the so-called Foulah plot revealed much the same elements as in all previous plots.

Although the Guinea government named France as one of the countries implicated in the Foulah plot, Guinean-French relations had been officially normalized in 1975 with an exchange of ambassadors. There had been an expansion of business of French firms operating in Guinea. For example, a new contract with Renault-Saviem for the purchase of 500 heavy duty trucks, tractors and buses had been signed; and an agreement had been made with Franco Rail for the reconstruction of the Conakry-Kankan railway. After the exposure of the Foulah plot, there was a noticeable cooling of relations between Guinea and France. In an attempt to placate Guinea, the government of President Giscard d'Estaing banned the publication of the newsletter of the Guinean exiles in France, and promised to keep a more watchful eye on their acitivites. In addition, he dismissed the notorious Jacques Foccart, whose secretariat was said to be the secret supporter of Guinean dissidents in Paris. Plans were made for the French president to visit Guinea. But relations deteriorated sharply again in June 1977 when

Alata's book 'Prison d'Afrique' was published in France, and the French press publicized it. Once again, the French government endeavoured to appease Guinea by banning the book; though it dodged the issue of extraditing Alata, informing Guinea that it was not within its power. He had apparently slipped away to Dakar.

The reason for the attempts by Giscard d'Estaing to establish friendly relations with Guinea at that time had much to do with the forming of a 'Francophonie' of French-speaking states, on the lines of the English-speaking Commonwealth prime ministers' conference with its permanent secretariat established in 1965. The idea had come from Canada as a result of nationalist fervour in the French-speaking province of Quebec. The suggestion was eagerly taken up by Senghor in 1976. Since the collapse of the French Community in 1958, there had merely been 'cooperation' between France and her former colonies, except Guinea, under which France maintained her interests on a bilateral basis. President Pompidou convened the first Franco-African conference in Paris in November 1973. But it was not until Giscard d'Estaing assumed power in April 1974 that 'cooperation' began to be transformed into a closer association. A second Franco-African conference took place in Bangui in March 1975. By then, membership had been increased to include the former French-speaking Belgian colonies of Zaire, Burundi and Rwanda. When the third conference took place in Versailles in May 1976, membership was extended to Comoros; and the conference was attended by observers from the Cape Verde Islands, Guinea-Bissau, the Seychelles, Sao Tome and Principe, states strongly influenced by French culture and the French language. A fourth Franco-African summit took place in Dakar in April 1977. There were representatives from Ivory Coast, Senegal, Togo, Upper Volta, Mali, Niger, Chad, Benin, Central African Republic, Zaire, Guinea-Bissau, Cape Verde, the Comoros, Rwanda, Burundi, the Seychelles; and observers from Djibouti. Eleven heads of state attended, and Zaire was represented by its foreign minister. Giscard d'Estaing was continuing de Gaulle's policy of trying to bring former Belgian colonies into the French fold. A few days before the conference opened on 20 April, French aircraft had just completed the Zaire airlift which enabled President Mobutu to defeat the revolt in Shaba province. French political and economic cooperation with not only Zaire, but with Rwanda and Burundi had increased to a point at which it exceeded that of the former colonial power. As might have been expected, neither Guinea nor the Congo were represented at the conference. Cameroon, Morocco and Mauritania also did not attend, though for different reasons.

Although the Dakar conference was scheduled to deal with economic matters, it in fact was concerned mainly with political issues. It appeared there was considerable support for the French airlift to Zaire. Giscard d'Estaing felt sufficiently encouraged to pledge 'unlimited French aid' to any country threatened by foreign intervention. When asked why France had intervened in Zaire, the French President replied: 'We have intervened in the Zaire struggle because we were asked to. I do not want African states friendly to France to feel abandoned. We want to give them a feeling of security and solidarity.' For this purpose, France maintains in France an elite parachute corps known as the 'force d'intervention', with an advance contingent stationed in Senegal. At the conference, Senghor went so far as to propose a *Force Africaine Commune* to be based in Ivory Coast, and to have the benefit of French logistical support.

This proposal, and the French government's later opportunism in supporting Mauritania against the Polisario front were regarded with great suspicion by other African states as manifesting France's ambition to re-exercise and extend her influence in Africa. France had become one of the largest suppliers of arms to the South African government; and had increased its trade with South Africa by some 280 per cent between 1968 and 1975, thus becoming a major investor in apartheid. The discovery of large oil deposits off the west African coast was seen as a further factor in moulding France's policies towards Africa.

Small wonder that the P D G strongly condemned the Dakar conference, and was extremely wary of French advances. By attempting to secure good relations with her former colonies and with other French-speaking states it seemed that the French government aimed to build the new French 'Commonwealth' through the African connection. In this imperialist scheme, Guinea presented one of the toughest challenges.

The success of the P D G in surviving the numerous plots to overthrow it may well have convinced the French that the P D G government, which rests on mass support and a collective leadership, is politically one of the more stable countries in Africa. Such stability cannot be discerned in some of the other former French colonies where the political complexion might change dramatically on the death of elderly francophone leaders. However, so fragile is the relationship of France with Guinea that the slightest trouble involving dissident Guineans in Paris awakens all the old mistrust.

The P D G expects its revolutionary policies to continue to make Guinea vulnerable to attack from reactionary forces both national and international. 'Whenever we reinforce the popular quality of the revolution; whenever we abolish petty privileges; whenever we attack the unlawful interests of a group; whenever we strike at the roots of injustice and exploitation, we have to expect an outburst of counter-revolutionary activity.'[20] Revolution triggers off counter-revolution.

The defence of the revolution still remains, therefore, a prime task of the Guinean people. As a result, the P D G continues to emphasize the importance of ideological education, maintaining that the revolution can only be successfully defended when there is 'perfect knowledge of the principles, and total and unreserved adhesion to the line of the revolution'.[21] Political training is not something that can be acquired once and for all. It must be continually developed as conditions change, and lessons are learned from experience.

Believing, with good reason, that it is perpetually under threat from reactionary forces, the people of Guinea are determined to defend their revolution, to radicalize and to develop it in solidarity with all peoples aiming to 'remould humanity to reflect the will of democratic progress and human justice'.[22] In the words of the militant P D G slogan, they are: *'Prêt pour la revolution.'*

9

INTERNATIONAL AND PANAFRICAN OBJECTIVES

THE P D G recognizes no separation between domestic and external objectives. International relations and panafricanism are considered, therefore, an integral part of relationships established within the nation founded on freedom, equality and democracy. In practical terms this has meant a foreign policy described as 'positive neutralism', and a radical panafricanism aiming at the total liberation and unification of the peoples of Africa.

In 1958, Guinea like most other states at independence, applied for membership of the United Nations, declaring its commitment to peace and non-alignment. Guinea was the ninth independent African state to join the U N. But in 1960, Africa year, seventeen new African states joined, and the Africa group formed the largest bloc in the General Assembly, accounting for about a quarter of its total membership. This together with the Asian group altered the whole balance of the U N General Assembly, the Afro-Asian bloc amounting to about one half of the total membership.

There had been a natural drawing together of countries which had a common history of colonialism. This had been shown in the Bandung Conference of April 1955, when for the first time, representatives of African and Asian countries met and declared their solidarity, and support for those still struggling to free themselves from foreign domination. It was a time when Afro-Asian solidarity and the non-aligned movement were bringing a new dimension to international relations, the emergence of a so-called Third World expressing the aspirations of the vast majority of the peoples of the world. These were for the most part the people of former colonies and the smaller states who had for centuries been deprived of any meaningful voice in world affairs, and who were determined not to be drawn into cold war politics.

The second Afro-Asian Solidarity Conference was held in Conakry in April 1960. Delegates from sixty-eight African and Asian parties and organizations took part. On the agenda were the complete abolition of colonialism in Asia and Africa; economic development; questions of social and cultural development; and the extension of the Afro-Asian solidarity movement. The permanent secretariat was extended by co-opting members from Algeria, Guinea and Congo (now Zaire). In addition, a 27-member steering committee was established to meet twice yearly.

For almost a decade, the non-aligned movement seemed the most attractive grouping for newly-independent states to join. In fact, for some it seemed the only possible line to follow if they wished to preserve their independence. But as events proved, it did not bring the expected advantages; and it began to lose its point and become confused as the cold war gave way to policies of detente. Nkrumah came to the view that the whole notion of a 'Third World' was a myth.[1] The term had come into existence when the cold war and the nuclear arms race was at its height, and when 'non-alignment' seemed practicable. It was, in essence, a revolt against imperialism and neocolonialism as basic causes of world tension and insecurity. With two power blocs of roughly equal strength, and poised it seemed on the brink of nuclear war, there appeared to be a reprieve for the world in the holding of a balance of power by some third force. However, as this threat receded, and the revolutionary struggle developed in Africa and Asia, the causes of world tension could no longer be viewed in terms of nation states and power blocs, but in terms of revolutionary and counter-revolutionary peoples. According to Nkrumah: 'the oppressed and exploited peoples are the struggling revolutionary masses committed to the socialist world ... They do not constitute a "Third World". They are part of the revolutionary upsurge which is everywhere challenging the capitalist, imperialist and neocolonialist power structure of reaction and counter-revolution. There are thus two worlds only, the revolutionary and the counter-revolutionary world – the socialist world working towards communism, and the capitalist world with its extensions of imperialism, colonialism and neocolonialism.² Nkrumah did not deny the existence of the struggling 'wretched of the earth', but maintained they did not exist in isolation. 'They are an integral part of the revolutionary world, and are committed to the hilt in the struggle against capitalism to end the exploitation of man by man.'³

Certainly, from the point of view of newly-independent states it could be expected they would find they had the most in common with the peoples of socialist countries. Where independence had been obtained as a result of armed struggle, the people's victory had been accelerated by their active support. In addition, capitalism was equated with colonialism and was unacceptable to those seeking a radical transformation of society. The point was put clearly by Saifoulaye Diallo, at the 22nd Congress of the Communist Party of the U S S R, in Moscow on 9 October in 1961. He was then political Secretary of the P D G and president of the National Assembly:

> Those who fight in a common cause against the same evil and for the victory of the same ideals are naturally in the same camp. Therefore, we declare that cooperation between the socialist countries and the young countries of Africa is a perfectly natural thing ... They (the delegates of the Congress) would understand better than others what significance Africa, exploited, colonized and humiliated, must rightly attach to the glorious revolution of 1917; and what hopes are raised among the peoples of Africa by your successes in the political, economic and social as well as technological spheres ... Revolutionary Africa knows that it can rely on the socialist countries.⁴

Countries of the socialist world had been among the first to recognize Guinea and to give assistance. But a much more important factor in shaping Guinea's predisposition towards the socialist bloc at independence was the P D G's commitment to a 'non-capitalist' path of development.

Independent Guinea's initial declaration of 'non-alignment', therefore, while it implied non-involvement in the East West power struggle, did not imply ideological neutrality. Furthermore, just as the term 'non-capitalist' was dropped as the Guinean revolution progressed, and 'socialism' was adopted to describe Guinea's domestic development objective, so also in the realm of international relations, 'non-alignment' was replaced by the term 'positive neutralism' as more accurately describing the foreign policy of the P D G. Positive neutralism is considered by the P D G to be founded on the following principles:

- honest cooperation with all countries
- respect for the sovereignty of all peoples
- non-interference in the internal affairs of other states
- refusal of any form of domination of one nation over another, a state over another state, a people over another people
- continuous reinforcement of the people's freedom of action and expression.[5]

The point is not to form a 'third force' between the power blocs, but to place foremost the common interests of peoples needed to speed up their pace of development. 'Small powers, wooed by the two major international currents of the rival blocs, have not yet succeeded in coordinating their efforts in order to uphold the common interests of their peoples. Yet these interests should be placed foremost if we want to harmonize rapidly the living conditions of all nations of the world.'[6] Positive neutralism then is founded on the right of each people to contribute to the general progress of mankind, and to take a fair share of all its fruits. In this stand, Guinea does not set itself up as a model, nor does it intend to fit into the mould of any other people, even a revolutionary people, though they may have common objectives. Every revolution is conducted against a unique political background: and this background has to be studied objectively in order to determine the successive phases and forms of action, methods of organization and tactics. 'In a word if indeed there is a revolutionary morale and revolutionary thinking, if there are indeed common objectives, their materialism is influenced by conditions linked to the stage of development achieved by each people in the context of its specific realities. This is why it should be understood that the revolution cannot possibly be imported nor given as a present. It is a living reality, translated into the thinking, conscious attitude and resolute action of all those who make it and who, gradually are transformed by it.'[7]

The P D G opposes all forms of exploitation, oppression and domination in Guinea, in Africa and in the world, 'because wherever they are found they imperil world peace; wherever they are at work they flout freedom and justice; wherever they are implanted they stand in the way of universal progress'.[8] The fact that Guinea does not take sides in a conflict should not be interpreted, therefore, as meaning that the P D G is neutral. Neutrality is a form of resignation that the P D G rejects. 'We want to shoulder the full burden of our international responsibilities ... We cannot possibly be neutral between good and evil, peace and war, justice and iniquity, progress and stagnation. If we resolutely refuse to align ourselves with this bloc or that ... we intend to make use of our rights as members of the international community in order to uphold what is fair and combat what is wrong.'[9]

The interpretation in practice of such terms as positive neutralism and panafricanism, which the P D G consider closely interconnected, illustrates the unique quality of the Guinean revolution. For the P D G's international policy is not conducted exclusively in the light of Guinea's interests but 'in line with, and strictly in conformity with, African interests'.[10] In fact, as far as the P D G is concerned, the interests of the African people as a whole override any consideration of a purely national character. According to Sékou Touré: 'Each time a problem arises in Guinea we seek a solution in line with African interests in general.'[11]

The total liberation of the continent and its eventual unification are objectives to be pursued in a positive manner. Guinea was among the first to send troops to the Congo (now Zaire) in support of a Lumumba in 1960. Since then, Guinea has supported the freedom fighters of the M P L A and

F R E L I M O in their wars against Portuguese colonialism. Guinea is the friend of the freedom fighters of Namibia, Zimbabwe and Azania; and also of the Palestinian people in their struggle to regain their homeland. But undoubtedly, the greatest contribution made by Guinea to the struggle against colonialism, has been the assistance given to the P A I G C. Since January 1963, when armed struggle was first launched by the P A I G C against the Portuguese in Guinea-Bissau, Guinea was a base area for the liberation struggle. It was to the P A I G C what Tanzania was to F R E L I M O. By December 1966, the P A I G C was able to declare that it had liberated more than half of Guinea-Bissau. In July 1967, Radio Liberation, the P A I G C broadcasting station, was inaugurated in Guinea as the armed struggle gained momentum. At the time of the Portuguese-led invasion of Guinea on 22 November 1970, when the headquarters of the P A I G C in Conakry was attacked, more than two-thirds of Guinea-Bissau had been freed. On 14 November 1972, the P A I G C was recognized by the U N General Assembly as the sole and legitimate representative of the people of Guinea-Bissau and the Cape Verde Islands. Less than a year later, on 24 September 1973, the independence of Guinea-Bissau was proclaimed at a meeting of the first People's National Assembly, in the Medina Da Boe region. Guinea was the first to recognize the new government: 'More than ever before, the Guinean people and their Democratic Party, and revolutionary government assure the brotherly people of Guinea-Bissaeu and the Cape Verde Islands, their party, the P A I G C, and their state council of their effective and militant solidarity in the military, material and diplomatic fields. Honour and glory to all struggling peoples. Long live the independence of Guinea-Bissau and the Cape Verde Islands. Long live the revolution.'

The total victory of the P A I G C which sadly its founder Amilcar Cabral, did not live to see, had in large measure been made possible by the steadfast support of the people of Guinea. In the course of the struggle, Portuguese aircraft on many occasions bombed Guinean villages and Portuguese troops made raids across the Guinean frontier inflicting casualties on the civilian population. But these incursions only strengthened the resolve of the people of Guinea to stand by the freedom fighters of the P A I G C. This resolve was never stronger than at the time of Cabral's assassination. If it had not been for the prompt action of Guinean forces, an entire section of the top leadership of the P A I G C might have been wiped out. After the murder of Cabral, Aristides Pereira and other leaders were kidnapped and put aboard boats which were to convey them into the hands of the Portuguese. But they were intercepted by Guinean naval forces and the prisoners were released. Sékou Touré and the P D G then instituted a full inquiry into the circumstances of the assassination, as a result of which the P A I G C was purged of fifth columnists who had managed to infiltrate the movement. The fact that the Second Congress of the P A I G C was held within six months of the death of Cabral, in the heart of the liberated territory of Guinea-Bissau, demonstrates the success of the P A I G C and P D G in overcoming what might have been a very severe setback to the liberation movement.

In a speech made at the symposium on the life of Cabral which took place in Conakry shortly after his death, Sékou Touré analysed the contradictions to be found within liberation movements, and emphasized the need for unity. In the case of the P A I G C, he considered the movement had been unwise in expressing in the choice of its name the 'double entity' of the struggle on the mainland and on the islands. He believed that the notion of a separation between Guinea Bissau and the Cape Verde Islands had played into the hands of the colonial powers who are always ready to exploit divisions.

The success of the P A I G C was one of the main reasons for the 1972 invasion of Guinea which in its turn sparked off the revolution in Portugal and the ending of the Caetano fascist regime. This was to have far-reaching effects on the western alliance, in Guinea-Bissau, and in Mozambique and Angola where liberation wars were in progress to end Portuguese colonial rule. It was the death blow to Portuguese colonialism, signalling the collapse of remaining military resistance to the freedom fighters of the P A I G C, F R E L I M O and the M P L A. The way was opening up for the final liberation battles to free Zimbabwe, Namibia and Azania.

Guinea's support for liberation movements remains open and unstinted. For the ultimate objective of the P D G's panafricanism is a totally free and unified continent. The Ghana–Guinea union formed in November 1958 showed the preparedness of the P D G to take practical steps in the direction of African unity. The process was taken a stage further in April 1961 when Mali joined the Ghana–Guinea Union and the Union of African States (U A S) was formed 'to work jointly to achieve the complete liquidation of imperialism, colonialism and neocolonialism in Africa and the building of African Unity'. Uninformed critics have scoffed at the Ghana–Guinea–Mali Union, their criticism being based on the false premise that the Union was intended to be an immediate, full-scale political merger or federation of the three states. This was not the intention. The Union would be initially a confederation, each state retaining its national personality but pursuing common policies on questions of mutual interest. The first steps to implement the Union would be the adoption of a union flag, and the harmonization of defence, foreign and economic policies. Subsequently, a constitution would be drawn up. The Union was at the outset, therefore, little more than a close treaty of alliance between radical states which would develop to form a nucleus for a political union of African states. As a first step towards a much wider unification, it was designed to demonstrate the practicability of political union. The fact that the U A S involved states from both the Commonwealth and French-speaking Africa made it of special significance.

It was becoming clear that relations between African states emerging from old colonial alignments were tending to be determined by the political complexion of post-independence governments. The Ghana–Guinea–Mali Union had shown that common panafrican and socialist objectives were stronger among progressive peoples than the relationships constructed during the colonial period. The parties led by Sékou Touré, Nkrumah and Modibo Keita, were committed to the total liberation and unification of Africa, and to programmes of socialist reconstruction. For them, panafricanism and socialism were synonymous, it being impossible to build one without the other. On the other hand, the governments of Senghor and Houphouët-Boigny, for example, placed emphasis on the continuance of close links with the former colonial power, and aimed to retain the social and economic structures of capitalism. Virtually all the French-speaking states, apart from Guinea and Mali, at that time consistently advocated a gradualist approach to African liberation and unity, insisting that economic and regional cooperation must precede any form of political unification.

As a result of the major differences between the political outlook of the peoples of radical and conservative states, two groupings of African states emerged in 1961. First, there was the radical group consisting of Ghana, Guinea, Mali, Libya, Egypt, Morocco and the Algerian F L N. This group was known as the Casablanca group after the Casablanca Conference held from 3–7 January. Secondly, there appeared the Monrovia group, comprising Nigeria, Liberia, Togoland, Sierra Leone, Somalia, Tunisia, Ethiopia and the twelve ex-French colonies known as the Brazzaville group. They were: Cameroon, Central African Republic, Chad, Congo Brazzaville, Dahomey, Gabon, Ivory Coast, Malagasy, Mauritania, Niger, Senegal and Upper Volta. The Brazzaville states held three conferences between October 1960 and March 1961, in Abidjan (October 1960), Brazzavillle (December 1960) and Yaounde (March 1961). At the Brazzaville Conference, the most important of the three, the states took the first step towards the setting up of a joint Afro-Malagasy Economic Cooperation Organization (O A M C E), and agreed to cooperate in economic, cultural and diplomatic spheres. At a further conference held in Tananarive, Malagasy in September 1961, a new joint Afro-Malagasy Union (U A M) was created which was to be open to all independent African states. Again, cooperation was to be to promote economic development and to safeguard their collective security. The U A M lasted until the formation of the Organization of African Unity (O A U) in 1963 made it superfluous.

The Casablanca powers and the Monrovia group had similar long-term aims in wishing to promote economic and cultural cooperation between African states. But they were poles apart on political and social objectives and priorities. This can be clearly discerned in the proceedings of their conferences. The African Charter of Casablanca provided for the establishment of a permanent African Consultative Assembly, and three permanent committees: the first political, the second economic, and the third cultural. In addition, there was to be a joint High Command. The ultimate objective of the Casablanca powers was an All-African Union Government, administering a totally liberated continent, pursuing socialist policies. In general, the Monrovia group envisaged a loose confederal type of union, with individual states retaining sovereign powers, and with the economic and social structures of capitalism. In other words, the class struggle was emerging as the determining issue. Progressive governments pursuing a panafrican and socialist path of development were grouping together; and those wishing to retain capitalist structures and pursuing policies of economic cooperation and bourgeois nationalism, were forming conservative links. Even when progressive and conservative groups got together sufficiently in 1963 to form the O A U, basic and incompatible ideological differences prevented meaningful panafrican solutions from being adopted; and the Organization has continued to fail to fulfil the aspirations of the African people.

Sékou Touré, like Nkrumah, envisaged an O A U with political machinery to provide a realistic basis on which the unification of Africa might be built. But right from the start of the discussions in Addis Ababa which led up to the signing of the O A U charter on 25 May 1963, it became apparent that differences between the African states were once again developing along the lines of the old power blocs and alliances. There were those who advocated a gradualist approach towards the unification of Africa, and wished to concentrate on economic and cultural cooperation; and those, like Guinea and Ghana which were convinced of the need for unified political organization to achieve continental liberation and economic development.

Nkrumah warned constantly of the dangers of Africa's continuing disunity in the face of mounting imperialist and neocolonialist pressures. At the second summit conference of the O A U which took place in Cairo from 17–21 July 1964, he again called for the creation of a Union Government of Africa. The specific areas of unified action would initially be defence, foreign policy and economic development, the latter implying a common currency for Africa and an African Common Market. Sékou Touré and the P D G supported the proposals which were in line with their own panafrican thinking. But once more, although there was general agreement within the O A U on the need for a Union Government, the matter was shelved for further discussion at the next summit conference, to be held in Accra in 1965.

As soon as the decision was taken to hold the conference in Accra, the governments of Ivory Coast, Upper Volta, Dahomey (now Benin), Niger and Togo declared that they would not attend. They used the excuse that Ghana was sheltering political refugees, and planning subversion in certain African states, though the basic cause of their opposition to the Accra summit was the fear that Nkrumah would at last succeed in persuading the O A U to adopt proposals for a Union Government. Although the opposition came from French-speaking states Guinea and Mali were among the radical states supporting political unification.

When eventually the summit conference opened in Accra on 21 October 1965, Nkrumah as expected, proposed the setting up of an Executive Council to act as the executive arm of the Assembly of Heads of State and Government. Of the twenty-eight states which attended the conference, twenty-two including Guinea, voted for the immediate adoption of the proposal. But a two-thirds vote of the entire O A U membership was needed, and it was therefore agreed that the matter should be referred back for further consideration to the governments of the member states. Some four months later, on 24 February 1966, a reactionary coup occurred in Ghana which toppled the C P P government, and Nkrumah accepted the invitation of the P D G to carry on the revolutionary struggle in Guinea.

The prompt action of the P D G in inviting Nkrumah to Conakry and appointing him Co-President of Guinea demonstrated the militancy of the people of Guinea and the strength of their panafricanism. They correctly saw the military coup in Ghana as an assault on the African revolution by 'the agents of imperialism'. The acceptance of the invitation by Nkrumah was in itself a great compliment to Guinea. Nkrumah knew that it was one of the very few countries in which he would be able to pursue his revolutionary objectives. When he arrived in Conakry on 2 March 1966, there began what he described as 'one of the most fruitful and happiest periods of my life'.[12]

From his arrival until August 1971 when he was compelled to leave Conakry for medical treatment in Bucarest, Nkrumah worked side by side with Sékou Touré, the P D G and the people of Guinea. During these years he wrote five books, four pamphlets, and made many broadcasts to the Ghanaian people.[13] He was in constant touch with African and world affairs. Freedom fighters, members of progressive organizations, diplomats and countless other visitors discussed their problems with him. He was in daily consultation with Sékou Touré, and members of the Guinea government and P D G. The African people will for ever be indebted to Guinea for protecting Nkrumah and for making it possible for him to continue his work. Undoubtedly, the close contact with the militant people of Guinea made a profound impression on Nkrumah. He never missed an opportunity to study at first hand the methods and organization of the P D G, and was particularly impressed by the party's vigorous socialist policies and its revolutionary preparedness. Nkrumah and the Ghanaians with him at Villa Syli underwent courses of military training with units of the people's militia; and regularly attended political meetings. On all important state occasions, Nkrumah could be seen at the side of Sékou Touré, his last appearance in public being his presence at the People's Supreme Court in January 1971 when the Guinean National Assembly met to consider the cases of the prisoners arrested during and after the invasion of 22 November 1970. Nkrumah was then a very sick man, but he insisted on being present to show his support for Sékou Touré on that very difficult occasion. It was appropriate that it was in Conakry that Nkrumah reached the height of his revolutionary stature.

Three days after he died in Bucarest, on 27 April 1972, the Guinea government had his body flown to Conakry where a state funeral and a symposium had been arranged. In a speech to the nation, Sékou Touré declared: 'the combatants of all races and colours, fighting for the independence and solidarity of all the nations of the world will continue to live and fight for Kwame Nkrumah's ideals'. He went on to state four conditions under which Guinea would allow the body of Nkrumah to be returned to Ghana. The request had been made by the so-called National Redemption Council (N R C) which had been set up as a result of a coup on 23 January 1972 led by Colonel Acheampong. The first condition was that the N R C should proclaim Nkrumah the 'legitimate president of the Republic of Ghana ... and rehabilitate the political and historic work of the great departed, in his struggle for Ghana's liberation and the emancipation and unity of the African peoples'. Secondly, all Nkrumah's 'comrades in arms' being detained in Ghana should be released. Thirdly, the ban should be lifted forbidding his 'comrades in arms' from returning to Ghana. Finally, that his body should be received 'with all the honours due to a head of state, and a funeral accorded to him worthy of his gigantic work in the service of all just causes'.

For two whole days, on 13 and 14 May 1972, ceremonies took place in Conakry to honour Nkrumah. The people of Guinea were joined by representatives of liberation movements, governments, progressive parties, trade unions and many other organizations. After a mass rally in the Conakry stadium, when for several hours units of the Guinean armed forces, people's militia, workers' brigades and women's and youth organizations marched past, the coffin bearing Nkrumah, draped with the Guinea flag, was taken to the mausoleum in a park in central Conakry. There it was placed beside the tomb of Guinea's national hero, Samory Touré.

Many hoped that it would remain there. But after some weeks of negotiations, the N R C succeeded in gaining the agreement of the Guinean government for its return to Ghana. It was reported that the decision was made as a result of the personal intervention of General Gowon, then Nigerian head of state, who was said to have appealed on behalf of Nkrumah's family. The coffin was flown to Ghana on 7 July 1972 on board an aircraft of Air Guinée. After a memorial service in Accra it was then laid to rest in the village of Nkroful, Nkrumah's birthplace.

As the years have passed, and more military coups have occurred, Guinea has become one of the comparatively few countries in Africa with a progressive civilian government. This has posed problems for the P D G. Military regimes are the very antithesis of peoples' governments. They have resulted from the seizure of power by armed force and they govern without a mandate from the people. Yet the P D G's panafrican objectives do not permit a policy of isolationism from such regimes. 'We will not undergo political events passively; on the contrary, we want to control their course and to steer them towards the higher political objectives that we assign to our political action.'[14] It is a militant policy which is essentially defined by the interests of the African masses.

In all too many African states, national liberation has not brought effective liberation of the people. These states proclaim their independence, 'but they place foremost the interests of the ruling class, which are at variance with the interests of the people'.[15] In not abolishing old feudal and colonial structures, they have entered into a new relationship with imperialism resulting in the imposition of a neo-colonialist state. Frequently, the objectives of such states are neither democratic nor rational; and personal and class interests, ethnic or even religious considerations are still preponderant. 'For all our feelings of brotherliness towards these countries and their peoples, we are nonetheless in contradiction with them on such issues.'[16] This, in practice, makes brotherly cooperation with them extremely difficult. Guidelines for PDG policy towards all African states, regardless of the political complexion of their governments, are based on support for the total liberation and unification of Africa. Therefore, 'first and foremost, we must make every effort for the total liberation of Africa, even if some of the prospective leaders of African countries seem to be reactionaries; beyond the policies that these leaders conduct, we must support their people's aspiration for freedom'.[17] Concurrently, the PDG strives to 'give a content to our quest for African unity, which of course is a means and not an end in itself. We do not want unity in confusion, but unity in action to satisfy the aspirations of the African peoples.'[18] Unless these twin objectives of liberation and union are actively pursued by all African states, the PDG maintains that the disputes and contradictions between them will develop and become fundamental, thus making the whole continent a vast area of conflicts which can only serve the interests of foreigners and privileged groups within Africa. According to the PDG, when a progressive step is taken by an African people, it is a step towards the liberation of Africa; and it weakens proportionately the forces of neo-colonialism. But every time an African government manages to cheat the people of a particle of their freedom, that government is growing increasingly subject to imperialism. The prospects for the African freedom struggle depend directly on the balance of forces between governments and peoples. When an African people makes progress in the direction of true democracy it inevitably draws closer to Guinea. On the other hand, those who conduct a policy of unequal rights, who do not respect the freedom and sovereignty of other states, and whose policy is in conflict with African interests, 'will not win our confidence'.

Guinea is prepared to associate with any governments or organizations if it considers such association is in the interests of the peoples of Africa. An example of this policy is Guinea's association with the European Economic Community (E E C). Although Sékou Touré and the P D G advocate an African common market, Guinea was a signatory of the Lome Convention of 28 February 1975 between nine members of the E E C and forty-six African, Caribbean and Pacific countries (A C P). The five year agreement established the largest trade area in the world consisting of fifty-five states with a total population of over 500 million. Three main concessions were won by A C P. First, there was established a system (S T A B E X) of guaranteeing the stablization of earnings from exports of twelve basic raw materials.[19] It was designed to be a form of insurance for A C P countries against bad years caused by the weather or a slump in world prices. Secondly, the Convention entitled A C P countries to refrain from giving any special trading advantages to the E E C; whilst the E E C was obliged to grant advantages to A C P countries. Thirdly, the Convention provided the forty-six A C P countries access to the European Development Fund (E D F). The Convention only came into operation after ratification some thirteen months later, on the first of April 1976. Then only 0.8 per cent of the E E C's total budget for 1976 was allocated to development 'aid', as against 4 per cent in 1975. The reason given for the drop was the oil crisis.

It is questionable, therefore, how beneficial association with the E E C is for the countries of A C P. A very low percentage of the 'aid' which does reach them is allocated for industry. Most of it is spent on the creation of infrastructure, or on pre-investment requirements for the securing of favourable conditions for the investment of private capital from the metropolitan countries. It smacks of colonial economics, and 'aid' with strings attached. In the words of Robert Marjolin, a representative of the E E C commission: 'Too often, donor countries have been pursuing selfish ends that have nothing to do with development; protection of their position of influence, stimulation of exports not of vital importance for the recipient country, short-term loans and credit at high rates of interest giving rise to an accumulation of debts that will prejudice the developing countries' financial future ... Let us also add general deterioration of trade terms to the detriment of the developing world.'[20]

Guinea's preparedness to associate with the E E C, and to be a member of the West African Economic Community (E C O W A S) can be understood within the context of the P D G policy of positive neutralism and panafricanism. It could be argued, however, that the very doubtful and limited benefits to be derived from either are a high price to pay for participation in organizations which undermine the creation of an African common market.

While it is not the policy of the P D G to concern itself with the internal affairs of other African states, the Guinea government is generous in the help it gives to peoples pursuing similar objectives. Apart from assistance to liberation movements, the P D G maintains a brotherly relationship with, for example, the M P L A government of Angola and the F R E L I M O government of Mozambique. On 22 November 1977, the Guinean ambassador in Maputo presented President Samora Machel with a chque for 900,000 escudos on behalf of the P D G.

It is Guinea's worthy ambition always to be a dynamic sector of Africa's evolution. The conditions under which the people of Guinea won their independence, the way in which they overcame their initial difficulties, and the progressive manner in which they are determined to solve the many problems confronting them, all are evidence of their contribution in speeding up the emancipation of Africa. A real community of identity and interests links all African countries though they may have very differing political and social structures. It may be described as a common culture, or personality; and it is this which the P D G seeks to build upon in order to achieve political union. The latter is made increasingly urgent by the requirements of the continent's economic development.

However, the African unity envisaged by Sékou Touré and the P D G 'does not mean that we should all become one; it is essentially a means ... of furthering Africa's development. It will be founded upon joint action for the achievement of some well-defined objectives which will influence in a decisive way the development potentialities of our respective countries, and give each of them a supreme guarantee of independence.'[21] Progress along the path of unity would consolidate Africa's independence, making possible her withdrawal from the sphere of influence of the great powers, and the full expression of the African Personality.

The panafrican cultural revolution expressing the African Personality has nothing to do with a racist concept of the African nation. It was born as a movement of revolt against colonialism and alienation. As such, it is a liberation movement which continues after the winning of political freedom. The achievement of independence merely provides the conditions for a reassessment of the entire question of 'development', which cannot be viewed in terms merely of economic growth. For the latter is meaningless unless it is firmly rooted in the cultural values of the people, the assertion of the African Personality and the delineation of the people's cultural identity. Négritude, which is a racist doctrine, is no part of it. The colour of the skin does not reveal anything of the inner man. It does not show his social class, his nature or his ideology. Revolutionary panafricanists are distinguished by their common commitment to African liberation and unification, in solidarity with the world socialist revolution. They aim to 'reafricanize' Africa after centuries of 'disafricanization'.

Objecting to the use of the word 'negro' Guinea refused to take part in the Festival of Negro Arts held in Dakar in 1966. 'Let's rather have an "African Cultural Festival", and we will have respected African unity. We will have freed the African personality. Those who before insulted us by calling US "nigger", and whom we fought against are the very people who today speak enthusiastically of négritude.'[22] In a statement explaining the P D G position, Sékou Touré said that négritude was a racialist concept of colonial times, and as such has no place in the new Africa. To talk of Africa in terms of colour is to try to divide the continent. The 1966 statement was reissued by the P D G when plans were being made for an 'African-Negro Arts Festival' to be held in Lagos. Sékou Touré referred to the Panafrican Cultural Festival held in Algeria when a resolution was passed condemning négritude; and he called for the Lagos festival to be named the Second Panafrican Cultural Festival. In the event the Lagos festival was called the 'Second World Black and African Festival of Arts and Culture' (F E S T A C '77).

In all foreign and panafrican issues affecting the interests of African peoples, Sékou Touré and the P D G can be relied upon to express positive and radical views which command great respect. For Guinea is known as a totally committed state fearlessly pursuing revolutionary objectives. There can be no better summary of these aims as far as Guinea's international policy is concerned, than that contained in Volume Ten of the works of the P D G entitled, *Africa on the Move:*

> Ours must be a militant diplomacy, constantly in keeping with the nature of our political commitment.
>
> We are not satisfied with the present international situation; we want to change it in a progressive direction. Neither are we satisfied with the current situation in Africa; accordingly we reject everything that contributes towards its maintenance and prolongation.
>
> Yet rejection is not enough; refusal is an essentially negative attitude; our action must constantly aim at modifying this situation, which affects Africa's historic interests and impedes the harmonious evolution of worldwide society.
>
> . . . . .
>
> Because we conduct a militant policy, we are not interested in the first place in making friends with this or that man; in establishing relations we are interested first and foremost in the value of their contribution to world affairs.
>
> Thus Guinea's international policy, which is simply the true prolongation of her home policy, is likewise defined in relation to the people's will and interests, and not by the quality of our relations with their governments ... All peoples should know that, in her international policy,

Guinea will never, under any circumstances, act against their interests.

Such are the guiding lines of our policy, the principle on which it is founded, the ideals which inspire it. But since political developments are essentially mobile, we must constantly analyse the situation objectively.[23]

10

THE PARTY STATE

Since its foundation in May 1947, the P D G has overcome great difficulties in its struggle for freedom and progress. Among its victories are the ending of colonial rule; the organization of the mass of the people on the basis of social justice and democratic freedom; and the creation of a revolutionary party-state which endeavours to exclude from the political, economic and social life of the country any arbitrary hierarchy. Through their high degree of revolutionary achievement, the people of Guinea are held in high esteem by all who aspire to similar objectives. Even those who are hostile, respect the integrity and courage of the P D G in continuing to pursue their independent line in the face of external and internal pressures.

However, the P D G would be the first to admit that much remains to be done. For example, there is need to broaden and consolidate the state sector of the economy. This is the basis of the national economy, on which political and economic structures largely depend. Unless it continues to expand, and private enterprise both foreign and domestic is kept within very strict limits, there remains the risk of the emergence of a privileged sector which could undermine plans for balanced, socialist development. Sékou Touré and the P D G evidently consider it worth allowing international monopoly finance to enter Guinea in order to speed up economic development. Therefore, like most governments of Africa and Asia, they are confronted with problems of how to maintain the country's independence and personality, while at the same time attracting the foreign investment needed for its economic development plans.

High on the list of priorities for the achievement of

economic independence are more industrial enterprises to provide basic goods for domestic consumption; and increased productivity of export sectors to yield more revenue for essential imports. While socialist production relations are improving the output of crops and livestock, rural production is still insufficient to make food imports unnecessary. Nor does it adequately supply the raw materials needed for industry and the export trade.

But while more exports are needed, and greater investment is required to increase productivity, great care has to continue to be exercised to avoid the danger of the foreign sector developing at a faster rate than the internal. For the P D G has rejected economic growth without development, since this would risk benefitting the few at the expense of the many. The party's objective is the full utilization of Guinea's own resources to ensure independent, balanced economic advance through decentralization, and policies involving the active participation of the people in their own development.

Though immense improvements have already been made in living conditions, housing, education, health services, communications and so on, there is still some way to go before the needs of the people are met. These are problems faced by a large proportion of the world's population. But in Guinea, material well-being is considered of secondary importance to political development and personal dignity and freedom. Therefore, economic development plans proceed at a pace consistent with the maintenance of the Guinean people's complete independence to manage their own affairs. While most countries at Guinea's stage of economic development would concentrate solely on achieving economic growth, Guinea sees the need to train political and technical cadres. For the active participation of all workers in the building of the nation's economy is essential if economic progress is to serve the people of Guinea and advance socialism.

There are problems caused by the continuing existence within Guinea of people with a bourgeois mentality, who believe neither in democracy nor socialism. These are the natural allies of neocolonialists and dissident Guineans living abroad. Some of them, posing as comrades, occupy important positions within the party. Sooner or later, the PDG aims to expose them as class enemies camouflaged within the party-state.

Then there are difficulties which the PDG attribute to 'indiscipline, waste, idleness, bureaucratism, parasitism and liberalism'. The party is constantly devising ways to eradicate them through programmes of political and cultural education, and through sessions of self-criticism when counter-revolutionary tendencies are analysed and discussed.

In the realm of international relations, Guineans seek to steer a way through East–West rivalries, while doing all in their power to bring about African liberation and unification. For the PDG sees African freedom and union as providing the only realistic solution for the fundamental problems of African nations. Through policies of pan-africanism and positive neutralism Guineans strive for world peace and the fulfilment of aspirations common to all peoples for freedom, justice and economic sufficiency. 'They are animated by the lofty and rightful ambition to belong to the community of the aware, hardworking peoples; to be in the vanguard of the social revolution in Africa and the world; to count among those people whose social values, thinking and human achievements inspire beyond their frontiers, the conscience of all men devoted to justice, brotherliness, solidarity and social progress'[1]

This is no mere rhetoric. In Guinea, the people are artisans of their own evolution. They therefore remain in a permanent state of mobilization as revolutionary processes develop and adapt to Guinean realities. Improvements are continually made to the 'line', for no static positions are taken. The political thinking of the people of Guinea is always in motion, within the framework of their strict adherence to the fundamental principles of socialism. Each party activist is an ideologist, a worker, a student and a teacher, expressing the party line in his behaviour. He transmits his ideas and knowledge to his comrades, and he learns from them. For the PDG, the accuracy of the line, the solidity of organization, and the loyalty of the membership are 'permanent necessities'.

At the beginning, the P D G was not so much a party as a movement opposed to feudalism and colonialism, which were then the dominant, negative elements in Guinean society. The people knew what they were against, but they had not then decided in a clear manner the line of development to be followed in order to achieve their liberation. In the course of time, the political party emerged to express in practical terms the collective will of the people for independence and a radical transformation of society. The P D G, therefore, in its first phase as a popular movement, and in its second phase as a political party, has always been based on the labouring masses, those who had nothing to lose in the liberation struggle, and who have everything to gain in the struggle for social progress. The party is the instrument which enables the people through democratic processes to decide the line of action to be carried out. It is an authentic expression of the people's class in the practical fight for democratic reality and equality.

Those who seek to place Sékou Touré and the P D G into some rigidly defined ideological slot will find it impossible to do so. Dialectical and historical materialism has had an important influence on the P D G's evolution, because the party has accepted the scientific bases of materialist doctrine. The P D G, however, retains its unique character determined by the mode of thinking of the Guinean people. For example, P D G policies reflect the fact that Guinea is predominantly an Islamic country, and that the majority of the people are profoundly religious. The party as a true image of the people contains nothing in its orientation or policies which causes anyone to suffer because of their religious convictions. Moslems, roman catholics, protestants and those without religion, all in a general way adhere to the philosophical basis of the P D G, and are fraternally united in the building of socialism in Guinea. Originally, there was some mistrust when the P D G was denounced by religious fanatics as a party of atheists. But this was overcome when the P D G adopted the tactics of itself organizing religious festivals. The party then began to introduce progressively the practice of democracy in the process of appointing imams to the mosques. After these initial victories, gradually other religious activities, not under the control of the party, were integrated within it. As the years pass and as the party progresses, religious factors may well decline in importance. This will be for ensuing generations to decide. For the time being, the P D G has based its doctrine on dialectical and historical materialism 'which is not at all contradictory to the Guinean people's conception'.[2] They have not, however, adopted the concept as interpreted by any other country, but as interpreted 'on the basis of the exigencies of the rapid evolution of the people of Guinea'.[3]

The step by step methods of the Guinean democratic revolution reflect the pyramidal structure of the party-state. This implies protracted and flexible processes of change as decisions made at P R L level are transmitted through districts and regions to central party structures. In this way, the people really do exercise effective sovereign power. It is the policy of the P D G to improve the workings of the P R Ls and their production brigades so that they may achieve maximum efficiency. For the P D G considers there is no more effective way in which the people can exercise power than through the local revolutionary authority. At the same time, district, regional and central revolutionary authorities must correctly interpret and carry out the will of the P R Ls, and make available to them the information which will help and guide them to make correct decisions.

The role of the leadership in the Guinean revolution is seen as expressing the aspirations of the people, and transforming them into revolutionary action. The leader must present all victories as peoples' victories, even though he may have played a vital role in the definition of the objective of the struggle, in the organization of the action, and in the effort which led to victory. He should never claim a victory as his own, or require any gratitude from the people. He is a product of the revolution, and not its originator. A competent, collective leadership is considered by the P D G to be an essential part of revolutionary organization. For one thing, the political consciousness of the leadership has the responsibility of promoting the political education of the masses. Obviously, there are varying degrees of awareness among the people. Party cadres and the national leadership take this into account when formulating policies for their consideration. Sometimes, theoretical formulation is ahead of the people's level of understanding or capability. Sékou Touré has, with characteristic simplicity, described in the following example the way to which the party leadership then proceeds:

> You tell some of your friends, 'Let's go to Bamako on foot'. Some would say, 'It will take us 100 days to reach our destination'. Others will bet 200 days. They are all scared by the distance and the effort involved. Ask them whether they are for progress. They will answer in the affirmative. Then invite them to go to Coyah (a town 50 kilometres distant from Conakry). They would readily agree, for they know that the journey would not take more than a day's walk. But before reaching Coyah, try to persuade them that Kindia is just nearby, and that there is more progress there than there is in Coyah. Once you are about to reach Kindia, you prepare them for another step towards Mamou. You tell them, 'Kindia has no electricity, but in Mamou you'll find plenty of it'. And their courage is renewed. Before reaching Mamou, prepare the next step leading to Kankan, and so on until you reach Bamako. All those who were originally opposed to the trip to Bamako will have been encouraged along.[4]

Although the dynamism of Sékou Touré permeates the Guinean revolution, and through it, the African revolution, there is no personality or leadership cult in Guinea. The achievements of Sékou Touré are the victories of the P D G. When he speaks he is the mouthpiece of the party. His political writings are 'the works of the P D G'. Everything he does is in the name of the party and the people of Guinea. While Sékou Touré clearly occupies a special place in the consciousness of the people, politicization is of such a high standard in Guinea that there is in fact genuine collective leadership. Sceptics, therefore, who wonder if the P D G can survive without the revolutionary activism of Sékou Touré appear to have underestimated the degree of the Guinean people's commitment to the policies of the P D G, and the efficiency of party organization.

The P D G has survived many attempts to overthrow it, the most dangerous being the 22 November 1970 invasion. Yet the underlying causes of the anti-Guinea plot still remain, and the people of Guinea cannot afford to relax vigilance. First, they seek to overcome the domestic base of subversion, and this involves strenuous efforts to eradicate reactionary elements within Guinean society. Some of these elements take encouragement from the presence of foreign capitalist enterprises in Guinea, and western diplomats who doubtless watch the situation very closely.

The P D G considers class struggle to be the 'dynamic of democratic revolution'.[5] It sees anti-feudal, anti-colonial struggles as forms of class struggle. Long before the P D G was founded, class struggle permeated Guinean society. With the formation of the P D G, it was intensified. It will continue 'to the point of transforming all the anti-people or counter-revolutionary elements for the benefit of the people's class, the revolutionary class'.[6] This will necessarily involve violence. For the P D G maintains that class struggle implies violence in some form or other. The exploitation involved in feudalism, colonialism and capitalism, is an intolerable form of violence. Imperialist violence includes methods of fascism, armed aggression and assassination. Bourgeois democracy, according to Sékou Touré, is 'a permanent violence in all respects: ideological, political, economic, social and cultural'.[7] Capitalism is violent, even if it does not undertake an open war of colonization, recolonization of neocolonization. 'It is profoundly violent when it imposes on the world the system of non-equivalent trade, the shameless system of exploitation of all the exploited peoples of the 'Third World', and of all the poor.'[8] It is violent even when those exploited do not openly resist because their resistance has been temporarily broken.

At a time when there is much publicity given to the violence of those struggling for freedom, it is well to reflect that violence has been employed far more for purposes of repression and oppression than for liberation. In the face of reactionary violence, progressive forces are compelled to use all forms of struggle, including armed struggle, in order to construct a just society. In the words of Sékou Touré: 'No true revolution can be conceived of without mass political actions, without coercive measures against the exploiters, without the installation of the dictatorship of the revolutionary classes, the people's class'.[9] Relations between social classes he sees as relations of violence in a latent or an active sense. No regime will just disappear in order to make way for another of an opposite nature without some form of violent process, even if the process involves no physical violence. Sékou Touré and the P D G regard it as a dangerous illusion to suppose that the people's class can, in certain conditions, take power from the bourgeoisie by what is customarily called the 'democratic process'. If the working masses succeed in acquiring power through a parliamentary election, they will be at some stage compelled to resort to violence in order to achieve genuine revolution. Otherwise, the international bourgeoisie will combine to disrupt the economy in order to regain power. The reactionary coups against the C P P government in Ghana, and the Allende government in Chile caused great shock in Guinea. Concerning the coup in Chile, Sékou Touré wrote: 'It was inadmissable to leave to the enemy of the people the exercise of power ... Once the people's class has conquered power ... it should not hesitate to resort to violence, if need be, against any reactionary who would attempt in one way or another, to jeopardise the full and sovereign exercise of the power of the people. The class enemy should not be given any respite'.[10] According to Sékou Touré, the P D G is fully aware that the building of a socialist state in Guinea involves violence, since it goes against the interests and the will of international imperialism, and its servants the local bourgeoisie.

Representing the working people of Guinea, the P D G as a party of the African democratic revolution has an historic mission to perform. It 'means to remain an African example of high quality in the full and complete exercise of political, economic, cultural and social sovereignty'.[11] The merging of the party and the state in the party-state is designed to express the people's sovereignty, exercised in every aspect of national life and at every level. It is not yet perfected. Democratic revolution is an evolving process, and the struggle continues.

Sékou Touré, on behalf of the people of Guinea has well expressed the task which lies ahead of the PDG: 'We must free ourselves from ourselves, from our old customs, old conceptions of life, our defects. We must free ourselves from the constraint that nature still exerts on us, and definitely control it. We must free ourselves from ignorance and sickness, and from all material and moral insufficiency. Self-liberation is synonymous with self-development ... Every day, the people of Guinea will be transformed; every day they will realize themselves still more, and this transformation can only be their own work.'[12]

REFERENCE NOTES

Chapter One

1 Quoted by Aimé Césaire in *Political Thought of Sékou Touré*, Présence Africaine, No. 29, p. 63.
2 He died while receiving medical treatment in Bucarest on 27 April 1972.
3 This chapter was written in October 1977.
4 Sékou Touré, *La Planification Économique*, Conakry, Imprimerie Nationale, 1960, p. 292.
5 The same, p. 95.
6 Sékou Touré, *Textes des Interviews*, p. 108.
7 Sékou Touré, *La Planification Économique*, p. 248.

Chapter Three

1 In French: 'Elève intelligent, assidu, ponctuel, mais un danger pour la France. En cas d'admission, l'orienter plutôt sur l'école Georges Poiret.' Quoted in *Ahmed Sékou Touré: l'homme du 28 Septembre 1958*, by Sidiki Kobele Keita, Professor of History at the Conakry Polytechnic. 2nd edition, 1977, p. 26.
2 Kwame Nkrumah, *Class Struggle in Africa*, Panaf Books, London 1970, p. 25.
3 The same.
4 Quoted by Aime Césaire in *Political Thought of Sékou Touré*, Présence Africaine, No. 29, p. 65.
5 The same, p. 66.
6 Blaise Diagne was in 1914 the first black African to represent the Four Communes in the Chamber of Deputies in Paris.
7 *Guinea under the Colonial System*, Présence Africaine, No. 29, p. 61.

Chapter Four

1 Pléven, Brazzaville Conference, 30 January–8 February 1944.
2 Edward Mortimer, *France and the Africans*, Faber 1969, p. 51.
3 The *notable evolué*, introduced by Eboué into A E F was recommended for other territories, with the suggestion that it could be extended to include artisans and skilled workers. The *notable evolué* represented, in effect, a new development of 'citizenship', which formed part of France's assimilation policy.
4 Mortimer, p. 51.
5 Mortimer, p. 50.

6 Sékou Touré, Vol. XXI, p. 72.
7 The same, p. 127.
8 The same.
9 Sékou Touré, Vol. XXI, p. 128.
10 The same.
11 The same.
12 Mortimer, p. 267.
13 *West Africa*, 13 April 1957.

Chapter Five

1 Sékou Touré, *The Political Action of the Democratic Party of Guinea for Emancipation in Africa*. Quoted by George Fischer in *The Significance of Guinea's Independence*, Présence Africaine. No. 29. English Edition, Vol. 1, p. 13.
5 The same.
6 Sékou Touré, Vol. XXI, p. 134.
7 They were Ghana, Ethiopia, Libya, Tunisia, Morocco, Egypt, Liberia, Sudan.
8 *West Africa*, Matchet's Diary, 30 August 1958, p. 820.
9 For details of this evidence of Nkrumah's practical panafricanism see Chapter Six.
10 Jacques Rabemananjara, in *Variations on the Guinean Theme*, in Présence Africaine, No. 29, pp. 88–9.

Chapter Six

1 *West Africa*, 8 Nov. 1958, p. 1067.
2 George Fischer, *The Significance of Guinea's Independence*, Présence Africaine, No. 29, p. 11.
3 Quoted by Aimé Césaire in *The Political Thought of Sékou Touré*, Présence Africaine, No. 29, p. 67.
4 Césaire, p. 68.
5 Kwame Nkrumah, *Handbook of Revolutionary Warfare*, Panaf Books, 1968, p. 35.
6 Proclaimed on 17 Jan. 1959, the Mali Federation was ratified by the Soudan Assembly on 22 Jan. 1959 and by Senegal and Upper Volta on the 28th. Upper Volta, however, soon pulled out. The name 'Mali' was chosen from the 14th century Mandé empire of Mali which had controlled the whole western Soudan from Cape Verde to the border of modern Nigeria. Its founder was Soundiatta Keita. Modibo Keita was descended from the same family.
7 The Conseil de l'Entente was a looser organization than the Mali Federation, being based mainly on economic cooperation between the member states.
8 They were Ivory Coast, Dahomey, Upper Volta, Niger, Senegal, Mali, Chad, Central African Republic, Congo (Brazzaville), Gabon, Cameroon, Togo.

9 De Gaulle, *Memoirs of Hope*.
10 The loan was to be made in four instalments at 2% interest, the sum of £1 million to be paid immediately, and the £3 million during the first quarter of 1959. Two further instalments were to be paid in 1960 and 1961.
11 Césaire, p. 71.
12 Alioune Diop, *Impressions of a Traveller*, Présence Africaine, No. 29, 1860, p. 8.
13 Sékou Touré, Vol. XII, p. 44.
14 Sékou Touré, Vol. VIII, p. 26.
15 From the text introduced by the P D G's Eighth Congress in 1967. A few changes were made in the Ninth Congress of 1972.
16 Sékou Touré, Vol. XI, pp. 165–6.
17 *La Guinée et l'émancipation Africaine*, Présence Africaine, 1959, p. 286.
18 *L'Expérience Guinéenne*, Présence Africaine, Présence Africaine, 1959, p. 286.
19 The same, p. 337.
20 *Class Struggle in Africa*, Kwame Nkrumah, p. 12.
21 Sékou Touré, Vol. XXI, p. 186.
22 The same, pp. 188–9.

Chapter Seven

1 Sékou Touré, Vol. V, p. 309.
2 Sékou Touré, Vol. XXI, p. 213.
3 The same.
4 Sékou Touré, Vol. XXI, p. 223.
5 Sékou Touré, Vol. X, p. 186.
6 The same, p. 185.
7 Sékou Touré, Vol. XXI, p. 226.
8 The same, p. 331.
9 Sékou Touré, R D A. No. 92, p. 215.
10 Egypt, Iraq, Libya, Saudi Arabia and the United Arab Emirates.
11 Samir Amin, *Neocolonialism in West Africa*, Penguin Books, 1973, p. 89.
12 Sékou Touré, Vol. XXI, p. 238.
13 A Susu word meaning elephant.
14 See Chapter 8.
15 Sékou Touré, Vol. XVII, p. 311.
16 Sékou Touré, Vol. X, pp. 482–3.
17 Sékou Touré, Vol. XXI, p. 192.
18 The same, p. 194.
19 Sékou Touré, R D A. No. 88, p. 19.
20 The same, p. 155.
21 Sékou Touré, Vol. X, p. 265
22 The same, p. 270.
23 *West Africa*, Jan. 1959, p. 242.

Chapter Eight

1 R D A No. 103.
2 His book *The Reds and the Blacks*, Hutchinson, 1967, pp. 16–17.
3 The same, p. 41.
4 Sékou Touré, Vol. XXI, p. 149.
5 The same, p. 151.
6 6/7 March 1966.
7 Sékou Touré, Vol. XXI, p. 153.
8 Kwame Nkrumah, *Neocolonialism: The Last Stage of Imperialism*, Panaf Books, Introduction, p. xi.
9 Speech by Nkrumah in the Accra National Assembly, 22 March 1965.
10 Published by Panaf Books in 1968.
11 Published by Panaf Books in 1970.
12 In a statement made to the Sofia correspondent of *Unita* on 4 Dec. 1970.
13 B B C monitoring report of Conakry broadcast 26 Nov. 1970.
14 Speech made on 26 July 1971.
15 Sékou Touré, Vol. XXI, p. 153.
16 The same, p. 155.
17 Speech to the militants of Conakry II, 14 Sept. 1973.
18 Brought to Conakry by a mercenary officer from Ivory Coast.
19 Sékou Touré, Vol. XIV, p. 197.
20 Sékou Touré, Vol. X, p. 157.
21 Sékou Touré, Vol. XXI, p. 398.
22 The same, p. 455.

Chapter Nine

1 Kwame Nkrumah, *The Myth of the Third World*, first published in 'Labour Monthly', Oct. 1968. Reprinted in 'The Struggle Continues', Panaf Books, pp. 74–7.
2 The same, p. 76.
3 The same, p. 77.
4 Report in *Pravda*, 26 Oct. 1961.
5 Sékou Touré, Vol. X, p. 593.
6 The same, p. 594.
7 The same, pp. 602–3.
8 The same, p. 577.
9 The same, p. 588.
10 The same, p. 542.
11 The same, p. 544.
12 Kwame Nkrumah, *Dark Days in Ghana*, Panaf Books, 1968, p. 19.
13 *Dark Days in Ghana, Handbook of Revolutionary Warfare, Class Struggle in Africa, Voice from Conakry, Revolutionary Path*. Pamphlets: *The Struggle Continues, Ghana: The Way Out, The Big Lie, Two Myths*.
14 Sékou Touré, Vol. X, p. 545.

15 The same, p. 552.
16 The same.
17 Sékou Touré, Vol. X, p. 553.
18 The same.
19 Groundnuts, cocoa, palm oil, cotton, coconuts, coffee, cotton, leather and hides, wood, bananas, tea, sisal and iron ore.
20 In an interview for *Le Figaro*, Oct. 1964, quoted in *Neocolonialism: Methods and Manoeuvres*, by Valery Vakhruschev, Progress Publishers, Moscow, 1973.
21 Sékou Touré, Vol. X, p. 584.
22 R D A, No. 88, p. 178.
23 Sékou Touré, Vol. X, pp. 544–5.

Chapter Ten
1 Sékou Touré, Vol. XXI, p. 606.
2 The same, p. 46.
3 The same.
4 Sékou Touré, Vol. XXI, p. 71.
5 The same, p. 72.
6 The same, p. 270.
7 The same.
8 Sékou Touré, Vol. XXI, p. 272.
9 The same, p. 273.
10 The same, p. 277.
11 The same, pp. 58–9.
12 The same, p. 278

From *Militant Poems* by Ahmed Sékou Touré.
R D A No. 21, English edition, Conakry, 1976.

TRIBUTE TO KWAME NKRUMAH

Returned to the country he has chosen
The body of President Kwame Nkrumah.
The grieving and sad people of Guinea
Gave him a unanimous and pure welcome,
A welcome full of strong and high moral intensity,
The man who embodied Africa
With passion, fidelity and courage
Against the forces of imperialism
Is now himself incarnated and honoured.
A whole people remember him
The People able to recognize true Merit,
Devotion and Efficiency of Man.
Death is still bound to happen, alas.
A human life is still limited.
Yet infinite Time and Space
By life valorized
For the benefit of People and History
Will give him a noble and great recognition,
Worthy of the Man and his Work.

Thus, the being he was, is and still remains
No longer in flesh, no more in blood,
But as Conscience, better as an ideal,
Sharing with force and constancy
The continuing struggle, dream of well-being.
Kwame Kkrumah belongs to those
Who have left a strong impact
On the destiny of liberty and dignity, loving humanity.
Kwame Nkrumah is and will be ever living
Since Africa, to him grateful
Is also living and will live for ever.
Fighters of all races and colours
Demanding Independence and progress for Peoples,
Equality and solidarity among nations of the world
Keep living and we shall continue endeavouring
To follow the path shown by Kwame Nkrumah.

If there are People of a particular time
There are also People of all times.
Kwame, the African, belongs to all times,
To all spaces, too.
Those who attempted to humiliate him

Only succeeded in glorifying him.
Indeed, time can neither soil his work
Nor tarnish his great and proud image.
In him is the Revolution
Which he is in.
Like the Revolution, he is 'transtemporal'.
Oh! Beloved son of our Peoples.
Friend of those who fight,
Enemy of those who surrender.
Kwame the worthy and courageous African,
The militant of the great Revolution,
You will be within us and with us
To revenge the martyrs, all the martyrs,
To liberate, unify and enhance the living,
To build Africa, United and beautiful.
Before your grave wherever it may be,
Fearless friends with militant faith,
With pure and faithful look
Will bow as a token of honour.
Your magnificence a hundred times will be exalted,
And glorified will be your unique contribution
To the cultural renaissance
And to the historical rehabilitation
Of those, all those who like you,
Have chosen duty and the struggle
Against blind submission.
Crushing down imperialism and colonialism
Is the duty you assign to us
Which will be assumed, fully assumed,
Nkrumah, our brother and our comrade;
Enemies will harvest shame
And Africa shall be to Africans.

30 April 1972

REVOLUTION

Global REVOLUTION!
You find the solution
For each of our pains
Darting forth lighthouse and compass
You guide together
Men and women, young and old
On the uneasy road of progress
Doing away with all hindrances
Step by step
Methodically and tirelessly
Organising persons, things
And means of struggle
In order to rebuild the nation
And better reconstruct the state
The family, the village and the region.

National REVOLUTION!
Your accelerated and assured move
Justifies your decisions
In their morality,
Always in compliance with human objectives
Controlling the vehicle of history
You unerringly orientate
All activities
Of the People, Nation and State
In perfect harmony and order
In the strengthening of their rational grounds
And in the certainty to forge victory.

Multiform but one REVOLUTION!
Reaction is under your feet
Mercilessly crushed down.
Forward, go forward
Without fear; without hesitation.
You are conscience,
You are action!
Men and women
Young and old
Have all in view
Exaltant plans
And have chosen
Means to achieve them
For the triumph

Of the People's cause
In order to meet
The just necessities
Namely:
Justice, equality, democracy and peace

Democratic REVOLUTION!
In front of you
Was standing the injustice stronghold
But henceforth
Woman is equal to man
And are born
The groundworks of the new community
In the family and the village
In the region and the Nation.
Beyond any privileges
Of age and sex
Of colour and faith
Will everywhere triumph
Equality, brotherhood and solidarity
For every one
To normally evolve
Within the communitarian frame
That is henceforth established
Both collective and individual.

Transtemporal REVOLUTION!
Heritage of past
Reality of present
Seed of our future;
It transforms both
Subject and object of history
Assigning to itself
Ever-growing objectives
To lead society
Towards its own surpassing.
For feudalism
Colonialism,
Imperialism
It has contempt and disdain
Its struggle against exploiting capitalism
Takes no end.
It wants to free society
From indignity
And makes it master of its own fate
A magnificent fate
That will be constructed
By the conscious efforts of all.

Economic REVOLUTION!
Source of prosperity
It exhorts the working masses
To produce more
To increase
The riches of the Nation.
It liberates the productive forces
As well as their initiatives
Organises co-operatives and trade unions
Whose dynamic activities

And progressive impulse
Will harmonise the interests
Through struggle,
A merciless struggle
Against selfishness and exploitation;
It suppresses under-development
Together with its share of insufficiency,
Misery and suffering.

Socialist REVOLUTION!
Starting from the People
For the well-being of the People
It socialises men
And their means of production
It nationalises the riches
Of soil and subsoil
In order to make inalienable
To domainal patrimony.
To any development
Assigning social objectives
It states the primacy
Of the People's right and interests,
To the People, it confers sovereignty and power
To the individual, freedom, participation and security
In order to assure interdependence
Between 'part' and 'whole'
Which belong to each other
And originate in each other.

Human REVOLUTION!
For which man is superior
To all material riches
Which by his work
He creates and censures.
It facilitates the bloom
Of intellectual faculties
Giving to the instruction
And the education of man

Their most human sense.
It guarantees for everyone
Liberty and dignity
In everyday life
Within society
Brotherly united
In solidarity.
It makes society human
And Being, universal.
And to the realms of love
Where angels dwell
It directs man.

Cultural REVOLUTION!
Free and enlightened thought
A sense of analysis, sense of synthesis!
From the earth
Man conquers space.
And the moon and the stars
Unveil the unknown.
Men in olden time
By their mystic creed
With its immutable horizons
Threw a gloom over universe.
Let us unite planets
Into a bunch of knowledge.
Let my faults grow into virtues
Past, present and future
Melt in the pot of action
In perpetual rebirth
Of ever new quality.
Born from time
And from my will
My intelligence is made sensible
And from the instinct proceeds my conscience
Which penetrates the infinite.
Man must steal from the sky its secrets
To see, hear and understand
The rhythm of the Cosmos.
Dead are reconciled with the living
We too, like you, wish
To live an eternal life
The life which is perpetuated
From generation
To generation.

Popular REVOLUTION!
Inexhaustible source

Of legitimacy and legality
Continue your onward move!
Necessary and useful
Serve the People and do not make use of it,
Your theory cast in action
Is exclusively based
On the capacities of the People,
The People,
Invincible and incorruptible
The true engine of progress;
Triumph over all forces of evil
And use conscientiously for your aims
Nature and science.
You are in my conscience and existence
The determining force
That enlightens and guides
My being
Towards a more beautiful future

Historic REVOLUTION!
Condition of the environment
Will of progress,
You make history.
You are even history
Which leads the slave
From colonial gloom
To the sunshine
Of freedom.
You enable the People
To perform the blissful transition
From irresponsibility
To full sovereignty
Which stops oppression
And degradation
Prosperous changes
Are thus brought about
For the progress of the People
On the road of time
And beyond continents,
Always onwards to happiness
On the endless horizon.

African REVOLUTION!
You have conquered me for yourself
For my People and for myself.
I understand your meaning
Just and irreversible.

I have committed myself to your line
Body and soul.
You have rendered confidence
To those who were about to fall in despair
Promoting without calculation
Everybody's condition.
For this very reason
You are in my consciousness
The reality
Which I belong to
In flesh and soul.
In my lifetime as in my grave
I entirely and for ever
Belong to you
Who are henceforth myself,
My People,
Their great ideas
Their courageous struggle
That must open
To unity.

PDG DATE SUMMARY

14 May 1947 First Congress establishing the PDG as the Guinean branch of the RDA.

20 Dec. 1947–19 March 1948 Railway Workers' Strike.

9 June 1950 General strike. Arrest of Sékou Touré.

15–20 Oct. 1950 Second Congress. Agenda: Party organization; worker-peasant alliance; the press.

1951 Election for Guinea's representation in French parliament. Candidates: Sékou Touré, Niankoye Samoo, former Captain Mamadou Dioudi Barry. Election rigged by colonial government to detriment of PDG.

2 Aug. 1953 Secretary-General of PDG (Sékou Touré), elected for Beyla as Territorial Councillor.

Sept–Oct. 1953 73-day general strike to obtain correct implementation of the Labour Code.

June 1954 Partial elections. Again, rigging against PDG.

9 Feb. 1955 The 'militant woman', M'Balia Camara, killed by colonialists in village of Tondon (Dubreka). This date marks the National Day of the Guinean Woman.

12–13 Nov. 1955 First Territorial Conference of the PDG, in Mamou.

2 Jan. 1956 Legislative elections. PDG invested Sékou Touré, Saifoulaye Diallo and Lansana Beauvogui.

Nov. 1956 Municipal elections. PDG victories in the 13 townships.

22–23 Feb. 1957 Second Territorial Conference, in Labé, to prepare for elections to the Territorial Assembly on 31 March 1957. PDG won 57 of the 60 seats.

14 May 1957 Secretary-General of the PDG (Sékou Touré) elected Vice-President of the semi-autonomous government, whose President was the colonial governor, M. Ramadier.

23–26 Jan. 1958 Third Congress, in Conakry. Structural reforms agreed: reorganization of the party; congresses to be held every other year; administrative reforms; suppression of indigenous provident societies; creation of administrative posts; suppression of discrimination in schools; health service made 'civil'; uniformity in taxation.

Election of a 17-member National Political Bureau.

May 1958 Plot uncovered which aimed to destroy new structures.

5–8 June 1958 Fourth Congress, in Conakry. Agenda: Launching of the popular movement called 'human investment'; the option for independence; youth organization; trade unions. Resolution passed calling for foundation of autonomous states in A O F and A E F.

25 Aug. 1958 General de Gaulle's visit to seek a 'Yes' vote in the September referendum on the French Community.

28 Sept. 1958 Guinea voted 'NON' in the referendum.

2 Oct. 1958 Republic of Guinea proclaimed an independent, sovereign state.

19 Oct. 1958 P D G withdrew from R D A.

1 Nov. 1958 Creation of Guinean National Army.

10 Nov. 1958 Constitution of Republic of Guinea adopted.

22–23 Nov. 1958 Ghana–Guinea Union created as a nucleus of a Union of African States (U A S).

12 Dec. 1958 Guinea became the 82nd member of the United Nations Organisation (U N O).

15 Jan. 1959 Second Congress of U G T A N, in Conakry. At this Congress, the trade union movement was defined as the determining factor of national liberation. Sékou Touré elected leader.

16 March 1959 Congress of Youth of the African Democratic Revolution. Defined role of youth on the basis of a single organization whose action was integrated into that of the masses organized within the P D G.

14–17 Sept. 1959 Fifth Congress of the P D G, in Conakry. Agenda: predominance of the party, and decolonization of structures and mentalities; sex equality; educational reform; suppression of private schools; economic planning.

1 March 1960 Creation of the Guinean currency as a special zone.

2–5 April 1960 Second National Conference, in Kankan. Three Year Development Plan approved.

April 1960 Second plot discovered to overthrow P D G.

Dec. 1960 Ghana–Guinea–Mali Union formed.

15 Jan. 1961 Presidential elections. Sékou Touré elected first President of the Republic of Guinea.

14–18 Aug. 1961 Fourth National Congress, in Conakry. Agenda: educational and banking reform; creation of state-controlled concerns.

27–31 Dec. 1962 Sixth Congress, in Conakry. Agenda: non-capitalist path of economic development; women's emancipation; the fight against mystification; judicial and administrative reform; creation of party federations.

15–18 Aug. 1963 Seventh Congress, in Kankan. Decisions taken: to renew legislative organs; 'purify' finances; create the National Council of the Revolution (N C R).

16–18 April 1964 Second Session of the N C R, in Gueckedou, to draw lessons from the Three Year Plan, and to decide on the Seven Year Plan.

14–19 Sept. 1964 Third Session of the N C R, in Conakry. Agenda: revolutionary firmness.

8 Nov. 1964 Promulgation of the Outline Law, which became the Charter of the Revolution. (Crack down on corruption and party members sabotaging P D G's socialist programme.)

7–11 June 1965 Fifth Session of the N C R, in Nzérékoré. Agenda: implementation of the Outline Law; establishing production targets; linking education to life; literacy.

15 Nov. 1965 Seventh Session of the N C R, in Conakry, to deliberate on results of the inquiries of the Revolutionary Committee concerning a military coup attempt.

2 March 1966 Arrival of Kwame Nkrumah in Conakry at invitation of the P D G. Appointed Co-President of Guinea.

27–31 Jan. 1967 Ninth Session of the N C R, in Labé. Agenda: establishing the People's Militia and Committees of the Defence of the Revolution.

25 Sept.–2 Oct. 1967 Eighth Congress of the P D G, in Conakry. Agenda: Radicalization of the Revolution; formal adoption of socialism.

30 Oct.–3 Nov. 1967 First session of the Central Committee, in Kankan. Creation of the Local Revolutionary Authority (P R L) in every village. Probing of assets and forfeiting of illegally acquired assets.

28–31 Jan. 1968 First National Congress of Guinean Women, in Conakry.

29–31 July 1968 Third Session of the Central Committee, in Kankan. Proclamation of the socialist, cultural revolution.

2 Aug. 1968 Launching of the 'radical revolution'.

27 Sept. 1968 Return and burial of remains of national heroes, Almami Samory Touré and Alpha Yaya Diallo at the Camayenne Mausoleum, Conakry.

9–13 Jan. 1969 Twelfth Session of N C R, in Conakry. Agenda: modification of statutes of P D G and C N T G; agricultural campaign; modification of structures of the Guinean People's Army; reorganization of People's Militia; twelve additional points to the Outline Law.

9–12 May 1969 Thirteenth Session of N C R, in Conakry,

devoted to consideration of attempt led by Kaman Diaby to overthrow P D G.

24 June 1969 Attempt to assassinate Sékou Touré by the mercenary Tidiane Keita.

Oct. 1969 All soldiers became civil servants. People's Militia increased.

22 Nov. 1970 Combined imperialist-colonialist aggression against Guinea.

1971 Investigation and sentencing of mercenaries and fifth columnists.

24–26 April 1972 Ninth Congress of P D G, in Conakry. Agenda: Radicalizing the revolution; election of Central Committee and Political Bureau of the Central Committee.

13–14 May 1972 Funeral ceremonies in Conakry for Kwame Nkrumah.

2 Oct. 1972 Tenth Congress of the PDG, in Conakry. Dealt with the Five Year Plan (1973–8); the defence of the Revolution.

13 Dec. 1974 Eighth Session of the NCR, in Conakry to deal with matters concerning the presidential and legislative elections of 27 Dec. 1974, and with modification of party statutes and the constitution.

16 Feb. 1975 Proclamation of the Charter of the Revolution. Dealt with class struggle; reforms of domestic trade which became the preserve of the P R Ls; closure of borders; creation of mechanized and animal-harnessed production brigades in all P R Ls of the party-state.

1975 E C O W A S formed. Guinea a member.

15–18 July 1977 Special Session of the C N R, in Conakry. Conditions stated on which Guineans living outside Guinea could return.

www.ingramcontent.com/pod-product-compliance
Lightning Source LLC
Chambersburg PA
CBHW061827300426
44115CB00013B/2280